January 13, 1993

To Josephine

Although a candle to you

I am still filled with a warm glow after our conversation which will, no doubt, inspire me to greater efforts in the future.

Warmest regards,

Victoria

WORKING
WIT OUT

WORKING IT OUT

THE WORKAHOLICS' SURVIVAL BOOK

VICTORIA McKEE

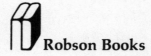

Robson Books

First published in Great Britain in 1991 by
Robson Books Ltd, Bolsover House, 5–6
Clipstone Street, London W1P 7EB

Cartoons by Larry

**British Library Cataloguing in Publication
Data**
McKee, Victoria
  Working it out: the workaholics' survival
  book.
  1. Employment
  I. Title
  158.7

  ISBN 0 86051 721 7

Photoset by
EMS Photosetters, Thorpe Bay, Essex
Printed in Great Britain by
Butler & Tanner, Frome and London

To my son, Daniel, and my daughter, Jessica, who are my greatest works

Contents

Acknowledgements

With many thanks to my husband, who has put up with my workaholic tendencies all these years (unless he's been too busy to notice), to my workaholic publisher, Jeremy Robson, and to *The Times*, *Sunday Times*, *Sunday Times Magazine*, *Sunday Express Magazine*, *Good Housekeeping* and *Options* magazine, which allowed me an outlet for my workaholic output and for which I did much of the research that led to this book.

With gratitude also to the workaholic specialists, such as Professor Cary Cooper (University of Manchester's Institute of Science and Technology), Dr Malcolm Carruthers (Positive Health Centre, Harley Street), Peter Grose-Hodge (Druces and Attlee), Paula Grayson (Luton College of Higher Education), Dr Desmond Kelly (Priory Hospital Group), Dr David Lewis, Christine McNulty (Applied Futures), Bob Tyrrell (Henley Centre for Forecasting), Dr John Nicholson (John Nicholson Associates) and Dr David Weeks (Royal Edinburgh Infirmary), who allowed me to call upon their expertise at odd hours of the day and night.

And, of course, to work enthusiasts everywhere.

Introduction

A Personal Perspective

'Who works for glory misses oft the goal;
Who works for money coins his very soul.
Work for the work's sake, then, and it may be
That these things shall be added unto thee.'
                                    Kenyon Cox

My name is Victoria McKee and I am a workaholic. I
don't collect stamps, make castles out of matchsticks,
play bridge, crochet cardigans or pothole. I don't even
have a secret lover (at least, not at the time of
writing!). My hobby is my work: I love it. Why isn't
that an acceptable admission for a woman to make?

After all, I'm a journalist whose brief is *life*. It's not as
if I'm a mortician obsessed with death, a drearily
calculating accountant or an insurance salesman who
can't stop selling in social situations.

I'm not even the sort of journalist to sell my
grandmother for a good story because I've got too
many irksome sensibilities not to respect others'
confidences above the opportunity for a 'scoop'.

So why do others feel threatened by the fact that I
enjoy working? Why is it OK to spend your weekends
sleeping, boozing, rambling, chatting, shopping,
shooting, fishing or chasing butterflies, but not to

spend them at your work, chasing ideas?

One Christmas my husband was furious when I wanted to make a single telephone call that pertained to work while we were visiting his family. But I found the call, which I eventually made (albeit from a corner call box while ostensibly out for a run) more exhilarating than a stultifying round of sherries and mince pies.

When I hit the telephone scant hours after my children's births, it wasn't just to spread the good news. Maybe – like many careerist mothers – I was over-anxious to prove I wasn't a write-off, but I couldn't confine myself to talk of babies and booties. I begin to twitch after more than two or three days out of communication on an exotic island paradise (unless I'm there specifically to write a travel piece), so I tend to choose holidays in major centres where news-worthy things happen.

Anyone's preoccupation can be an irritant to others – particularly to family members who feel neglected by it. But surely mine is no worse than my husband's with sport, my son's (at the time of writing) with Teenage Mutant Ninja Turtles, or my neighbour's with gardening?

A certain degree of workaholism is expected of those at the top, where the lines between business and pleasure blur and mergers are made on the golf course. To me the concept of not mixing business with pleasure seems crazy, but then, my business is pleasurable.

I can remember sipping champagne at a press launch of a new product a couple of months after the birth of my first child, when a male executive double-edgedly praised my 'bravery' for coming back to work so soon. 'Bravery?' I said incredulously. 'This is easy. Staying at home full-time with the children would be the hard work.'

I still fully believe that, and have nothing but admiration for those with an affinity for that most demanding, twenty-four-hours-a-day, seven-days-a-week job – which can lead to its own form of workaholism and encompasses, as some shrewd insurance companies have noted, the equivalent of numerous other jobs, such as nurse, cleaner and psychologist.

Male workaholics are better tolerated in society partly because they usually have women dedicated to servicing them – 'executive wives' meant to share their involvement by hosting corporate dinner parties and attending 'social' functions, as well as making sure that their clothes are pressed and their home and family life are as wrinkle-free as possible.

When a man is the breadwinner, a wise wife quickly learns on which side hers is buttered. Women bringing home the bacon don't have nearly such a jammy time.

There seems to be an expectation that women, even if they work, will derive the lion's share of satisfaction from human relationships and spend their spare time flower-arranging or decorating cakes. But I'm afraid I'm the odd man out at mother and toddler groups, and would rather donate £10 than spend all day sorting jumble to raise maybe £3.98 for the school funds. I have little time for charity work (even the kind that begins at home) or the other intriguing projects in which my friends-who-are-at-home seem to get involved.

Someone once asked me if I *had* to work. I had never

even considered the question. I had been raised, by a workaholic father and a mother who took just two weeks off from her own business to attend to my birth, to believe that people – men *and* women – had careers which provided them with personal fulfilment, rather than jobs to pay the bills. My father regularly popped into his office on a Saturday, 'just to check the mail', and found the holidays my mother forced on him pure purgatory. He used to say that the truly lucky ones were those who could earn a living doing what they loved. Well, I've been privileged to know that joy – even if I've missed a few others along the way.

I'm not pretending money doesn't matter to me, but I can honestly say that I've never worked *for* it. I work out of some inner compulsion, and if I could pause long enough to discover what fuels my drive, I'm sure the discovery would make fodder for another feature (or maybe even a book!). I landed several jobs in my youth simply by saying, 'I'll work for nothing just to gain experience', and I still forget to invoice employers for work done and expenses incurred because I'd really much rather be working on the next idea than being pedantic about pounds and pence – even if that policy isn't always cost-effective.

Sometimes when I'm working flat-out on a story, I can be up until 3 am without realizing it: time flies when you're having fun.

I don't want to give the impression that I'm a total social misfit. A large part of my work as a journalist involves socializing, and in my admittedly infrequent off-duty moments I enjoy jogging and swimming, going to the theatre, taking long walks with my husband, nattering with friends, days out and about with the children, browsing and shopping, reading and watching television, cooking, dancing – and 'you know what'.

But I don't spend hours over my make-up, afternoons under the hair dryer or weeks in health farms – unless, of course, it's for a story. And, frankly, I find my work more rewarding than crying over spilt milk, wiping sticky fingers and refereeing fights over which cartoon video to watch next. (I get enough of that as it is!)

I know some people will be wondering what on earth I had children for if I didn't want to look after them. But I reason that if I can pass on to my children the gift of being able to earn a living while doing what they love, I may not have done too badly.

This introduction is more or less the text of an article I had published in *Options* magazine in June 1989, the year I began my investigations into workaholics and the society that seemed to spawn them.

If you have taken time out of your busy life to read this far, might it be that you, too, are one? Or are you merely intrigued by the phenomenon of workaholism and its future in the workplace – and the world – as we work our way, with greater or lesser enthusiasm, towards the third millennium?

Either way, I hope you will read on.

1

Workaholics Unanimous?

'No man is born into the world whose work is not
born with him.'
James Russell Lowell

Workaholism can destroy lives, as the enterprising
entrepreneur Jane Young discovered to her cost in
1987, when she won a 'Businesswoman of the Year'
award but lost her husband and baby – and eventually
even her company – in the process. (Her husband ran
off with the cleaning lady who had time to look after
him, a miscarriage was blamed on overwork, according
to newspaper reports at the time, and bankruptcy
court beckoned.)

Workaholism can also save lives, as former Prime
Minister Margaret Thatcher proved when working
into the wee hours kept her from almost certain death
or serious injury in her bed during the Brighton
bombing. The latest thinking suggests that it may
even prolong lives – hence the schemes afoot in both
Britain and the United States to offer life-enhancing
employment to people past the arbitrarily defined
'retirement' age. Witness Mrs Thatcher's apparently
increasing youthfulness and vigour while in office.

So, is workaholism a disease, to be regarded in the same light as alcoholism, or a desirable syndrome which should be encouraged in a productive society? And will everyone's attitude towards work require a radical overhaul as we teeter towards the third millennium?

I called this book *Working it Out* for a number of reasons. Work attitudes need working out, by individuals and by organizations. Workaholics may be working out hidden agendas which should be brought into the open. Also sometimes simply working out, through a favourite exercise, sport or pastime, can help us all to work more effectively. And, if I'm being totally honest, I hoped a lot of people would pick it up thinking it was an exercise manual! It is a 'survival book' in the sense of being about the survival of a species, and how we may all – workaholics and work-ambivalents alike – have to adapt to survive in the workplace of the future.

A workaholic is generally regarded as someone who works not always wisely or too well but always too *much*. Ask an artist to draw one and the picture will probably be of a drudge whose desk is piled high with papers he (and it will undoubtedly be a 'he') can clearly never hope to shift. Or the workaholic may be noticeable by his *absence* – as in the British Telecom advertisements of the late 1980s depicting a child's drawing of his family, in which his workaholic Daddy never featured. The image struck a powerful chord with British managers, 75 per cent of whom, according to Telecom's research, believed they were working too hard, to the detriment of their family life. (One of those surveyed remembered how his young son, who had come to meet him at the airport, was asking all the men who came off the plane, 'Are you my Daddy?') Ironically, the advertising executive who dreamed up the advertisement – for BT's 'Workplan' business communication scheme, supposed to let the phone take the strain – was apparently inspired by his own failure to appear in his child's drawing of a family scene. And the psychologist involved cheerfully admits that he's a workaholic too.

The classic caricature of the workaholic executive – largely drawn from American films of the 1960s – is of a pill-popping coronary case with a peptic ulcer. My definition encompasses actors and artists, authors and athletes – anyone who is immersed in their work with intense commitment.

Take Adrian Moorhouse, the champion swimmer. He told me, when I interviewed him for the *Sunday Express Magazine* in 1990, how he had even put romantic relationships on hold for the sake of his sport. 'When I stop swimming, maybe I can slip back to normality,' he reasoned.

Most of the self-confessed workaholics I have met are vital, dynamic people who simply love what they're doing so much that it doesn't seem like work to them, so they are incapable of 'downing tools' or turning off at 5 pm. And most of the vital, dynamic people I have met consider themselves – or are considered by those around them – to be workaholics. Their work is usually creative, and they get a buzz from it.

The campaigning actress, author and gardener Susan Hampshire says, 'Gardening, waterskiing and my work are the three most enjoyable recreations in the world to me – and I look on my work as a recreation. I love it! My husband calls me a workaholic, but I don't think of it like that.' (Even the rigours of a lengthy provincial run with *The King and I*, away from home comforts and living on late-night curries and greasy fish and chips had failed to dampen her enthusiasm for her work.) Or the totally dedicated fashion designer Zandra Rhodes, who revels in the quiet times – like over the Christmas holidays – when she can really get down to some serious work, uninterrupted, and goes only on 'busman's holidays', to promote her designs or get inspiration for them, she once told me.

As a journalist I have done hundreds of interviews with happy, well-adjusted high-achievers who professed to be workaholics – while at the same time chronicling the high levels of stress and stress-related illnesses said to spring from a supposedly overworked society. Through my writing on marital and family issues, I have encountered relationships that were put under enormous pressure by workaholic tendencies in individuals and organizations – as well as those which were enriched and uplifted by a love affair with work. In writing articles on management styles and motivation I noticed that the qualities companies were attempting to engender in their employees (often through macabre motivational manoeuvres such as weekend war games) were those which many workaholics instinctively possessed – but that workaholism was condemned as a disease or an addiction.

So I became fascinated with what constituted the difference between the dynamos and the drudges, why one group thrived while the other barely survived, and what we could *all* do to acquire the enthusiasm and energy of the former without the danger of 'burning out', like the latter. Also, as an

American who has been resident in Britain for many years, I keep a keen eye on transatlantic developments that might shed additional light on what is happening here – sometimes illuminating the way ahead, sometimes showing us all too clearly which way *not* to go! Through my interviews with psychologists, 'futurists', management consultants, doctors and stress specialists on both sides of the Atlantic a picture began emerging of aspirational – and practical – working patterns for the future.

While a workaholic rubbish collector or traffic warden might understandably appear to verge on the neurotic, in a successful actor, writer, politician, chief executive or entrepreneur a certain degree of work-aholism is *de rigueur*. And show me a successful self-employed person who is *not* of workaholic persuasion!

A report issued in 1990 by the National Westminster Bank, which runs a Small Business Service, showed that entrepreneurs either had, or quickly developed, a workaholic streak. 'Entrepreneurs are willing to make significant sacrifices to achieve their major objectives of independence, job satisfaction and financial reward,' a spokesman noted. Three out of four worked harder than when they had been in employment and the same proportion also earned more. And – most significantly – while two-thirds of the 2,000 owners of small businesses surveyed admitted to a strain on their relationships with their partners because of the long hours worked and increased responsibilities, and half said they spent much less time with friends, four out of five affirmed that they would still choose to be their own boss if they had to make the choice over again. One, who had started a successful sports and leisure company, lost his steady girlfriend in the process because he never went out in the evenings any more, but added, 'You can't beat being your own boss'. A fashion retailer rowed with her husband and abandoned her social life because of the long hours she spent at work, but asserted, 'It was all worth it. I love the work and am in control of my own destiny.'

The neglected partner and/or children of a workaholic may have good cause to complain – and many lives appear to have been ruined and marriages wrecked by a preoccupation with work to the detriment of personal relationships. But in such cases it is usually the *emotional unavailability* of the workaholic that is the problem, rather than the amount of work, and the underlying issue needs to be worked out. One woman I know – herself a very successful journalist in a demanding job – is in no doubt that workaholism is what killed her marriage to a fellow hack. He used to seek out increasingly more dangerous, long-distance assignments and, when he was home, closet himself with his typewriter and remain emotionally unavailable to his family.

When in 1990 I was interviewing the award-winning playwright Robert Bolt for an article in the *Sunday Times Magazine* on his struggle to speak and write again after a stroke, his wife, actress Sarah Miles, told me that in some ways she actually *preferred* her husband as he was now, in comparison to the driven workaholic he had been. She enthused: 'He is much more open now than he was. He can see all around, whereas before he just saw ahead of him. He was always talking so fast or writing! The man was a workaholic and they are extraordinary creatures, as you might know. I was never allowed to interrupt him or knock at his study door unless there was fire or pestilence. He'd be in there from five o'clock in the morning until six at night, and since he was a lark and I was an owl we never saw each other. I was so riveted to know what he might be doing that I once crawled up the mill we live near and went right around until I could see the window where I knew he would be working with his back to me. I was clinging on with my fingernails, watching in fascination. He'd go from whisky to cigarette to chip butty to coffee and screw up pieces of paper and then the whole routine all over again like a ritual. The pain of creation! Now we're having a garden room built and then we'll play chess there until the twilight comes . . .'

She was happy to have her husband emotionally available to her in a way he hadn't been when he was physically fit. Then, Bolt confessed, he had been able

to divide his mind easily among several things. Now he had to concentrate on just one – and to his wife, when she was that one, it was rewarding. And funnily enough, Bolt felt he was nearly as prolific as he had been in his workaholic prime, although now he could sit at his word processor only in the mornings, instead of for a full day, typing with one hand and fighting to find the right word.

If someone is shutting out their family and friends to an unacceptable degree, it is probably *personal* relationships they need to come to terms with, not their work. Is the wife of a workaholic any worse off than, say, a 'golf widow'? Of course, many wolves masquerade in workaholics' clothing, using the guise of workaholism to cloak their tawdry affairs, so that 'working late' and 'on the job till all hours' for them take on quite different connotations. And many people would rather their partner was having a love affair *with* the office than *at* the office – a state of affairs one American academic, Dr James Martin, predicted would become increasingly common in the 1990s, when, he suggests, there will be an un-precedented explosion of office romance.

I am not attempting to minimize the strains that an unreasonable and obsessive workaholic can create for those around him or her. But these are strains which any obsessive personality, whether obsessive about appearance, housework, sport or whatever can engender. The housewife who will never sit still but continually sets herself tasks to perform, or the ardent hobbyist, may be in many ways, a closet workaholic. Take Beryl Armstrong, an amateur novelist and film-maker who was written up in the *Telegraph* magazine in early 1991. She is also a keen miniaturist – building, decorating and furnishing an amazingly detailed doll's house – and an enthusiastic member of her local bonsai-growing group. Sometimes, admittedly, obsessive workaholics are obsessive in other areas too. They may drive themselves so hard because they are perfectionists, for whom, as Dorothy Rowe, author of *The Depression Handbook* (Collins, 1991), puts it, 'every achievement is a failure'.

The wife of the hard-working cancer specialist Professor Timothy McElwain, who committed suicide some time after it was suggested that the report he co-authored on the Bristol Cancer Help Centre was inaccurate, told the inquest that her husband had been 'a perfectionist', while a colleague told the court the professor 'had suffered a complete loss of confidence' when his work and the professional reputation he had spent a lifetime building were attacked. This could be seen as a supreme and tragic example of what can happen when people identify too completely with their jobs, or are driven by something besides mere work enthusiasm.

Bernadette Vallely, the intensely workaholic co-founder of the Women's Environmental Network, says she is quite convinced that workaholics come from families which are 'dysfunctional' in some way. However, this conviction doesn't dampen her enthusiasm and almost missionary zeal for her work in the environmental movement. She is usually at her desk early in the morning, stays ridiculously late at night and takes work home for evenings and weekends. If her motives were anything but noble, she would be in a different job earning a lot more money for her efforts. The idea that workaholics come from 'dysfunctional' families is so commonly voiced that there must be elements of truth in it. However, many of the world's greatest achievers have come from families which could be considered 'dysfunctional', and I will be rash enough to suggest that 'average' families are more likely to produce 'average' people.

Any tendency when pushed to its most extreme limits can seem eccentric, and Dr David Weeks, author of *Eccentrics: The Scientific Investigation* (Stirling University Press, 1988), found many workaholic eccentrics among his sample group, some of whom I visited for a feature I was writing on the subject for *The Times*.

There was Alan Fairweather, for example, a botanist who worked as a potato inspector for the Department of Agriculture. He was totally pre-occupied with potatoes in his off-duty hours too, existing almost completely on a diet of them, reading books about potatoes and planning pilgrimages to the International Potato Centre in Peru.

Then there was Russell Eberst, the information officer for the Royal Edinburgh Observatory, who kept three computers in his sitting room to track the thousands of satellites sent into orbit since he first became fascinated by them with the launch of Sputnik2 over thirty years ago. Although his wife, Margaret, knew of her husband's love affair with astronomy when she married him, she admitted that she had had no idea quite how all-consuming it would be, or how much it would affect her life. On their wedding night her husband got up at 3 am and insisted she share with him the excitement of the conjunction of Mercury and Venus! The Ebersts went on to produce three children, each of them with an obsessional interest that they looked likely to turn into a career. They boasted, quite justifiably: 'At least we've never had children who didn't know what they wanted to do!'

Dr Weeks discovered that the obsessive focus of eccentrics not only made them oblivious to the irritations and stresses of daily life but helped to make them generally healthier, happier and longer-living than the supposedly 'normal' population. Some of what he found true for them would, I suspect, hold true for workaholics too. But where do you draw the line between an acknowledged 'eccentric' like Russell Eberst and an admittedly obsessive work enthusiast like Cliff Cowburn, a fourth-generation butcher, profiled in *You* magazine in 1991, who claims to wake up in the middle of the night crying out new combinations of sausage seasonings, and admits that he also daydreams about new varieties of sausages and would eat them at every meal if his wife allowed him to?

Basically, the well-balanced workaholic who manages to maintain a healthy grip on human values as well as a passion for work is unlikely to suffer, or cause anyone else to suffer (too seriously), as a result of his or her work enthusiasm.

On learning that I was writing a book on workaholism, however, Susan Hampshire told me that she thought many women used work to cover up an essential loneliness. 'You are creating something that is very fulfilling in some ways,' she said reflectively – speaking of all creative women rather than herself specifically – 'but that doesn't mean that when you've finished creating the garden or the book or whatever and you sit back with a glass of cool white wine and a sense of accomplishment you don't wish X was there with you to share the moment.'

She thinks she became a workaholic, she explained, because her husband, the impresario Eddie Kulukundis, is also a 'man of many passions', as she put it, 'who has interests in so many areas – sport, the theatre – that I thought if I don't fill my life up with interests, if I was waiting all the time . . .'

An American report published in 1989 indicated that divorced women did better than their married counterparts in the business world – possibly because success in work was regarded as a compensation for failure in marriage (a phenomenon explored in more detail in Chapter 6). Conversely, workaholism can lead to marriage breakdown – particularly when the workaholic is a woman who is not always 'there' for her man.

Like so many committed career women, Jennifer d'Abo, chair of the Moyses Stevens Group, attributes the breakdown of her relationships with men to her dedication to the job. 'I married three men who all expected to have a wife who'd take care of them in a traditional way,' the successful tycoon – who insisted she would never marry again – told me. 'I was never given any quarter because of my work. I was also too busy to accompany my last husband to Ascot and Henley – and he found that boring.'

Jackie Staples, founder of the mail-order fashion business Jake, freely admits that the pressures and perks of running her own successful company played a significant part in her marriage break-up.

'Sonia', an executive secretary, enraged her husband by the amount of attention she lavished on her boss and the sense of responsibility she had – despite her low salary. Many devoted secretaries end up marrying their bosses because they bring the nurturing qualities associated with the ideal wife into the working environment, a combination that appeals to the workaholic male chauvinist. (If the secretary then becomes housewife and is distanced from day-to-day office affairs, she may find she loses some of her appeal.)

There is evidence that the family that works *together* works out. Workaholic parents produce workaholic children, who often create close-knit family dynasties in which business is animatedly discussed around the dinner table and no one would dream of drawing lines of demarcation between business and pleasure. Such families hark back to ancient times when you were called Thatcher or Baker because your father, your father's father, etc. had been thatchers and bakers, and there was a total sense of identification with the job that went beyond the need to work hard for a living. They worked with the love that distinguishes the craftsman from the production-line worker.

It is a tradition, for example, in the Lalaounis family of goldsmiths (who have what they refer to as 'galleries' all around the world) that every new baby must be brought to the family's studio in Athens to touch gold-dust before they go home from the hospital, Ilias Lalaounis's daughter Katerini told me.

All three of his beautiful daughters were cast in the goldsmith's mould. 'My father brought us into his workshop when we were babies and I did the same with my children. My father just absorbed us into the business – we've been involved since we were three years old. Now we are taking over,' Katerini said proudly as she watched her children – born with golden spoons in their mouths – cutting their teeth on expensive ornaments in the Bond Street shop.

Most of the world's great family business empires have been built on workaholic foundations and continue to foster those principles, even though there is technically no longer any need for them.

'We love our work,' the Marchesa di San Giuliano Ferragamo told me for an article on the Ferragamo dynasty in *The Times*. The Marchesa, who clearly doesn't *have* to sell shoes, continues, together with the rest of the Ferragamo family, to have an intense and active involvement in the dynastic business. After her father Salvatore's death, her mother, Wanda, became *presidente* of the board, her brother Ferruccio managing director, her sister, Giovanna took charge of the women's fashion collection, her brother Leonardo became menswear supremo, her sister Fulvia was responsible for accessories and her brother Massimo for the New York operation. She filled her father's shoes as chief designer.

They regard it, insisted the Marchesa (named Fiamma, possibly because she was meant to carry on the 'flame' of her father's enthusiasm and be the torchbearer to future generations), more as 'a sacred trust' than a business – although business was doing nicely, thank you. Her father, she said, believed that his children should be taught to love their work as much as he did. She was sixteen when her father pulled her, the eldest daughter, out of school to learn the trade at his side.

'I always thought I would go back and continue my education,' she confided. 'But there was a feeling of destiny in following in his footsteps.'

Sir John Harvey-Jones, brilliant businessman that he is (and a well-balanced workaholic, who tries to

keep weekends and holidays as family time), seemed
to miss the point of some of the family businesses he
went to advise for his excellent BBC television series
Troubleshooter in 1990. Some of the people he saw gave
the impression that they couldn't have cared less
about optimum profits – they were having *fun*
working the often outdated and inefficient way they
were, and telling them that they could make more
money if they sold off the loss-making but most
enjoyable part of the business was not what they
wanted to hear.

At the time of writing, Lord Hanson's son Robert is
associate director of his father's company, Robert
Maxwell's son Kevin runs the publishing side of
Maxwell Communication Corporation, acting dynasties such as the Redgraves, the Cusacks and the
Oliviers are flourishing – and acting *together* – and Flora
and Rebecca Fraser have followed the penprints of
their prolific mother, Lady Antonia Fraser, and
grandmother, Elizabeth, Countess of Longford, who
are both the authors of numerous long and pains-
takingly researched works of historical biography
which require great discipline and determination to
produce. (The study of family businesses, dynasties
and variations on a similar working theme within a
family would merit a book in itself.) Lady Antonia
once told me: 'Flora has inherited the workaholic gene
from my mother. I think it skipped a generation with
me.' However, her many admirers are not convinced of
this, and methinks the lady doth protest too much.

In any case, such workaholism must not be
confused with the grinding drudgery of the Dickensian
drone who of necessity toils away for long hours to
make ends meet, or that of the Uriah Heeps of this

world, who like to give the appearance of working long hours in the hope of being thought better workers than they are. Workaholism for such ulterior motives is not true workaholism at all; to work extra time for extra money is an entirely different matter. The factory shift worker who greedily opts for every overtime hour doesn't qualify, nor does the moonlighter who juggles three jobs in order to pay a particularly high mortgage or save up for a special holiday.

A workaholic – in my book – is someone who works for a motivation other than money, even if financial success is a welcome by-product of their endeavours. (The actor Kevin Costner described the feeling in an interview in the *Daily Mail* when he remembered how he first marvelled, 'This is so incredible. I'm doing exactly what I want and I'm getting paid!')

Fame may be the spur, or a desire to prove something to themselves and to others, or the work may be a displacement activity which masks a deeper desire to feel loved or needed. But if the motivation is *external* rather than internal – that is, a desire to be *thought* successful or to keep up with the Joneses – then it is probably somewhat superficial, and such people would not count as genuine workaholics, since they would thankfully abandon their work once the objective was achieved.

True workaholics are driven from within, either from a pure enthusiasm for and constant curiosity about their chosen field or from a deeper need to prove something to *themselves*, so that no matter how much money they had, they would still continue to work (even if, perhaps, at a slightly more leisurely pace).

The successful comedienne Ruby Wax told the *Daily Mail* in 1991 that her workaholic drive stemmed, she was sure, from trying to prove to her parents that she could be successful. 'It's the only-child syndrome. And the fat, ugly-child syndrome. Fame is revenge against those who never believed in you,' she said with admirable candour.

It has been noted that many women who have scaled the heights of achievement have had – like workaholic former Prime Minister Margaret Thatcher – the powerful pull of a successful father figure with whom to identify and emulate. The MP Leo Abse went so far as to suggest in his unflattering biography of Thatcher, *Margaret, Daughter of Beatrice* (Jonathan Cape, 1989), that Mrs Thatcher's disdain for her housewife mother 'left the Prime Minister a driven woman, forever desperately working out her private travails on the public stage'.

Researching for my article on the subject for *The Times* in 1989, I discovered that many women who had become successful in non-traditional fields, over-coming obstacles with a steely determination, had felt closer to their fathers than their mothers. Mary Archer – scientist, former don and the first woman to be elected to the ruling council of Lloyd's – told me then, 'Of course one can only speak from one's own experience, and I think rejection is too strong a word. But like many women who've been fortunate, I have had a very supportive father, particularly when I chose science, which I suppose is considered quite a masculine subject – although I feel hesitant to describe it as such because so many of the qualities in science are neuter or abstract.'

Dr Rosalind Miles, author of *Women and Power*

(Futura, 1986), *A Woman's History of the World* (Michael Joseph, 1988) and numerous other books on women and work, confirmed: 'Women of power always need to locate themselves in the male line because power is traditionally male.'

One of the many articles which have been written comparing and contrasting the influential editors Anna Wintour and Tina Brown (of, at the time of writing, American *Vogue* and *Vanity Fair* respectively) made the point that 'both had aloof, successful father figures who shaped their early psychological make-up . . .'

That said, does it really matter whether someone is working out of an overpowering desire to please a dead father or better an ineffectual mother if they genuinely enjoy their work and are productive in it? 'Not in the least,' several experts have assured me – as long as their work makes them *happy* rather than unhappy, and they don't feel they are constantly striving to live up to standards they can never meet. Many have accused Wintour of setting standards that are too exacting for those who work with her to live up to. Her early-morning exercise sessions, impeccable appearance at the desk by 8 am and other workaholic habits, which may have been at home in New York, were alien to the laid-back British 'Voguettes' even in the mid-1980s. And Tina Brown, whose exercise trainer arrives around 6.30 am, told the *Telegraph* magazine just prior to the launch of *Vanity Fair* in Britain this year, 'I like operating under pressure. Then I can forget myself. It's the same reason I never wrote the novel I said I would. Sitting on my own, tormented by introspection. Yuk.'

The happiest workaholics are undoubtedly those

who are motivated by the sheer enjoyment of their work and a belief in its intrinsic value. Even if this overlaps with a hidden agenda they are also working out, they are as different from the drudges and the desperate, driven drones as the connoisseur of fine wines is from the alcoholic.

If workaholism is an avoidance tactic which prevents the worker from working out more serious problems, then it is worrying. If it keeps someone from their family and friends, or, more significantly, from *themselves*, then the workaholic obviously needs help, even if he or she is oblivious to exhortations to seek it – or too busy to stop and consider them.

As Bertrand Russell is reported to have said, 'One of the symptoms of an approaching nervous breakdown is the belief that one's work is terribly important.'

But the workaholics who are actually 'workafrolics' – as one workaholic personnel consultant likes to think of herself – or 'work enthusiasts' (an American coinage credited to a Professor Janet Spence of the University of Texas and meant to cover those who love their work with a passion but have enough passion left to love other things – and people – too) are undoubtedly a gift to the world.

Where would we be without the supposedly 'absent-minded' (actually work-obsessed) scientists who have made so many great discoveries at the expense of exploring personal relationships? As Thomas Alva Edison, inventor of (among other things) the electric light and phonograph, discovered, 'There is no substitute for hard work.' He believed that 'Genius is one per cent inspiration and ninety-nine per cent perspiration.'

Trouble brews when those who are not born

workaholics have workaholism thrust upon them – by a macho and masochistic corporate culture of the kind developed and disputed over several decades in the United States, and which finally and firmly took root in Britain in the 1980s.

As *Fortune* magazine described it, 'A new corporate style dubbed the "high commitment" model has sprung up, suggesting ominously that your life should revolve around work and not much else.' Many reluctant and worn-out workaholics have confided to me over the years that they feel trapped into putting in long hours for the sake of job security or keeping up appearances in a high-pressure profession. This is an entirely different matter, and strategies for getting off such a thankless treadmill will be discussed in later chapters, when we will see how the worst elements of workaholism can be weeded out for a more fruitful future.

The 'high-tech, high-stress' 1980s were a time when technology made twenty-four-hours-a-day working possible for the first time. Portable telephones, paging systems and faxes made it difficult for the switched-on ever to turn off, and the accoutrements of urgency were suddenly chic. An awesome stress-relief industry sprang up to cope with the side effects, pushing everything from electronic biofeedback devices (which replaced the simply aesthetic 'executive toys' of the 1960s) to juggling classes. Corporate counselling became commonplace and purveyors of 'personal services' promised to live your life vicariously for you while you worked. And you had to work hard to afford what they charged to walk your dog, iron your shirts, pick up your children, deliver calorie-counted gourmet meals to the door and coordinate your Christmas shopping campaign. But the climate, contends Bob Tyrrell of the Henley Centre for Forecasting, is changing. The pencil and the blank piece of paper are what the avant-garde are bringing to meetings now, rather than briefcases bulging with technological wizardry, and at least the *appearance* of leisure will once again become fashionable, he predicts – as has been the norm for centuries. (Remember how the white skin of Southern American belles was prized because it demonstrated that they had no need to toil in the sun like 'rednecks'? The long, curling fingernails of Chinese mandarins had similar symbolic significance and in some cultures plump wives were prized because their girth made it obvious that they seldom stirred and were supported by men of financial substance.)

But there is a concurrent, conflicting trend: whereas workaholism was once a middle-class affliction and prerogative – unnecessary among the leisured classes and incomprehensible to the working – as Britain moves increasingly towards the sort of melting-pot meritocracy and 'celebritocracy' of the United States, what you *do* is beginning to matter even more.

The latest social stratification systems show that you are what you do these days, and that people define themselves increasingly by their jobs. It was always considered the American way to look at where you could go rather than where you had come from – the American dream that any child could aspire to become president – while in Britain where you came from carried more clout than anything you could ever earn. But with a trapeze-artist's son following the grocer's daughter as Prime Minister, preaching a 'classless' society in which 'people are not blocked off from anything merely because of their background . . . because of where they came from', the pressures associated with aspiration and upward mobility have been enhanced.

Since 1911 the Office of Population, Censuses and Surveys has altered its Register of General Social Classes into a breakdown of social class as defined by occupation – class 1 being professional, 2 managerial and technical, 3n skilled non-manual, 3m skilled manual, 4 partly skilled, 5 unskilled. And since 1955, according to Lord Justice Denning, the concept of the 'working class' has been 'inexplicable'.

Even so, in 1990 the Duke of Westminster was able to successfully invoke an ancient clause in the lease on a block of flats on his patch which specified they were to be made available only for 'people of the working class', despite the protests of the more plebeian Westminster Council leader Lady Porter. Although the hard-working aristocrat won his case and made his point, Paul Keers pointed out in an article in the *Daily Telegraph* before the verdict, that 'the shoeshine boy, for instance, once a street vendor, is now a young entrepreneur with initiative . . . and so the working class – those who are actually working, that is – have been absorbed into the bright new world of the professional class. And left at the bottom of the social order is the *non*-working class. As John Mortimer puts it, "Today you are either middle class or sleeping in a cardboard box."'

According to a revised 'dictionary' of 1,500 jobs and professions published by the Market Research Society in Britain at the dawn of the 1990s, a public-school-educated young man on a high salary could be rated a

C2 if he was doing a manual job, such as shoving Ming vases around in Sotheby's basement, and a duke's daughter would merit only a C1 if she was working as a secretary and maintained her own flat. The uneducated – even uncouth – head of a large sewage company employing over 200 people could be considered an A, together with leading judges, barristers and senior civil servants, one of the compilers of the dictionary explained to me, while a girl from a good family with a university degree would be rated D if she was working – albeit temporarily – as a groom. C2s – skilled manual workers such as plumbers and electricians – were on the whole a richer group than C1s – minor clerks and clerics, etc. – and it is not only the profession but the *stage* of that profession you are in which determines your grouping. 'A young doctor might be a B while a senior consultant would be an A, a village librarian a C1, a librarian in charge of a large branch library a B and a chartered librarian who was the head of a whole library system an A,' my informant explained.

So it is official (theoretically, at least): wealth and family background count for little any more in the new order. The job almost completely defines the person, so changing job changes social status – as has been the case in the more mobile American society for centuries.

In an age where pop stars rub shoulders with princesses and Royals participate in television romps (remember the dreadful *It's a Royal Knockout?*), even aristocrats suddenly seem eager to be thought members of the working class – as the recent BBC television series *Working Titles* demonstrated. The Earl of Lichfield has long been a photographer, his sister,

Lady Elizabeth Anson, a party planner, the Earl of
Bradford a restaurateur, the Duke of Marlborough's
daughter Lady Henrietta Spencer-Churchill at the
time of writing runs an interior design business,
Princess Margaret's son is a carpenter, the Princess
Royal has jockeyed for position in the horse world, the
Princess of Wales's brother Viscount Althorp is a
transatlantic television presenter (and the Princess
herself once worked in a kindergarten), Prince
Charles's former flame Lady Jane Wellesley is a
successful television producer, Prince Edward is a
thespian, the Duke of York a working (well,
supposedly) sailor and his Duchess professes to
continue to work in publishing, the Countess of
Woolton (like Lady Sarah Armstrong-Jones) is an
artist, the Earl of Mount Charles a rock concert
entrepreneur – the list of working titles goes on and
on. Some, like the Countess of Woolton, who paints –
often ten to twelve hours a day – under her maiden
name, Sophie Birdwood, hide their titles out of fear of
being thought merely debby dilettantes.

Wealthy matrons treat their charitable commitments
with workaholic fervour, and 'gels' from good homes
who were once raised only to be ornamental are now
seeking careers for credibility. And not just those who
come from families dubbed the *'nouveaux pauvres'* in
Nicholas Monson and Debra Scott's amusing book of
the same name, although the 'downward nobility', as
Monson and Scott call them, are learning the
advantages of upward mobility.

Professor David Cannadine, in his controversial
book purporting to chart *The Decline and Fall of the British
Aristocracy* (Yale University Press, 1990), insists that
the aristocracy has been reduced to the working

classes out of necessity. But this was hotly disputed around the book's publication, partly because there has been, since the 1960s, a growing feeling that *noblesse* obliges an interesting occupation – and not merely for second sons.

The 1991 edition of *Debrett's People of Today* has removed what it considers 'superfluous gentry' in order to include more self-made achievers. So, as the *Sunday Times* observed, 'out go Viscount Encombe, Lady Rose Cholmondeley and the Hon Carolyn Ponsonby . . .' in favour of 'Paul Gascoigne, the footballer, Vivienne Westwood, the avant-garde fashion designer and Jocky Wilson, the darts player. A place has also been found for Martin Jacques, editor of *Marxism Today.*'

And since it is possible to acquire a title through work – as the prolific author P D James and innumerable others have demonstrated – the distinction between working titles and titled workers is beginning to blur.

Queen Noor of Jordan – the former working architect and urban planner Lisa Halaby, who runs her own Foundation and numerous other projects – told me in 1991, 'I am a workaholic, there's no question. When I married it never occurred to me that I wouldn't continue to work.' Unlike our own Royal Family, which seems to place a high priority on holidays, the Jordanian one 'hasn't had a family holiday in three years', the Queen told me without a hint of self-pity.

Princes of Wales have problems, it has long been suggested, because their only 'job' is to wait and train for the job to which they have been born. Which brings us to 'vocations'. If I may coin (I believe) a phrase, those with vocations seldom take vacations. Or do they? Can the Pope ever claim to be 'off duty', even when hiding out at his secluded Castel Gandolfo retreat? Would Mother Teresa put her feet up at weekends?

And just when does a career qualify as a vocation? According to *The Concise Oxford Dictionary*, it doesn't have to be religious or charitable; it just requires a 'sense of fitness for a career or occupation'. So someone can quite justifiably argue that acting, or journalism, or running a multinational company is, for them, a vocation which needs to be nurtured in almost every hour God sends.

A recent survey – and surveys, of course, can demonstrate just about anything – noted that a high proportion of successful top executives rely on hunches and instincts which stem from an intrinsic belief in themselves and their 'vocation' for the job which lesser managers lack.

The young Laurence Olivier (a shining example who spurred me on to my earliest workaholic excesses, which included scrubbing out toilets in 'summer stock' theatre companies at the age of twelve and spending my summers slaving, as an unsalaried, starry-eyed dogsbody with the New York Shakespeare Festival) believed his reverend father would expect him to feel a vocation for the church. But when he dutifully suggested following in the paternal footsteps, the perceptive Reverend Gerald Kerr Olivier told his son not to be so silly and that his vocation was, quite obviously, to be an actor.

Olivier, even in his later years, never overcame his actor's insecurity, his widow Joan Plowright recalls. He *needed* to work, even when he might quite easily have rested on his considerable laurels. It wasn't just the money, as she explained on BBC television's *Wogan* show in 1990, that made her husband accept what many people considered such dreadful roles in his old age. There weren't many great parts for old men, she rationalized, and that great old man needed to feel himself a working actor to the end.

Finally, the stereotype of the workaholic is male. For women, who have to work twice as hard thanks to their invisible 'second shift' of housework and childcare, as the American Dr Arlie Hochschild describes it in her book of that name, there is much less understanding and support.

This book is an attempt to examine, through anecdotal and expert evidence, the workaholic individual and culture, to distinguish between the dynamo and the drone, and to work out a more balanced blueprint for the future – as I am trying to do in my personal life in the supposedly more humanistic, holistic 1990s.

As a journalist I cannot fail to acknowledge that this book is biased, since it sets out to be a defence of a creature too often caricatured and condemned. But I hope there is something in it not just for those who live to work but for those who would like to do more than work to live – and those who live or work with those who live to work.

2

The Workaholic Ethic

---

*'If all the year were playing holidays, to sport would
be as tedious as to work.'*
William Shakespeare

You can always tell a workaholic by the way he or she
is willing to let the children scream, the dinner burn
and the spouse seethe while animatedly talking shop.
Workaholics volunteer their home telephone (and fax
and mobile phone) numbers, whereas nine-to-fivers
sound really shocked if you suggest trying to contact
them outside office hours. And while some people go
on holiday and try to pass it off as a business trip,
workaholics go away on business trips and pretend
they are holidays.

A workaholic is someone whose life really *wouldn't*
change on winning the pools, and who will find a way
to work in the labour ward or the casualty ward. If
they have the sort of work they can pursue even while
laid up, it spares them the withdrawal symptoms
experienced by the workaholically dedicated RAF
wing commander, who agonized when brought back
from the Gulf to recuperate in a British hospital from
severe injuries, 'I am really concerned that I will leave

my squadron behind. I feel I am deserting them.'

As a journalist I naturally collect workaholic contacts, like Professor Heinz Wolff of the Brunel Institute of Bio-Engineering, who is happy to discuss his latest space or scientific programme on a Sunday, or to expound upon the wonders of workaholism on a weekday night. Professor Wolff can barely stand to take a day off, since his brilliant brain is always buzzing with new ideas. 'I don't like going to parties or travelling to exotic places on long holidays,' he once told me. 'Maybe to people who don't do much all week a change is as good as a rest, but to someone like me who's busy all the time a *rest* is as good as a rest.' His wife sounds cheerfully resigned, and it must have been clear from the start that she was marrying his work as well.

Then there is the broadcaster Jimmy (now Sir James) Savile, of *Jim'll Fix It* fame, who is such a workaholic that he keeps no fewer than nine homes – some of them mobile or merely a room in a hospital – around the country so that he can always sleep 'over the shop', so to speak, when he's working – which he is constantly. Since he is single and unencumbered by family commitments, he can immerse himself totally in his work – much of which is for charity. He doesn't seem to work for the money, although he does enjoy some of the trappings of wealth, such as Rolls-Royces, big cigars and gold-lamé tracksuits. His loyal and obviously also workaholic secretary is on 'twenty-four-hours-a-day call' to coordinate his extraordinarily complicated diary, and his Christmas and New Year's Eves are spent stalking the corridors of Stoke Mandeville Hospital, dispensing jollity to paralysed patients.

And what about Jilly Forster? Together with her
husband Rob Lamond, she is (at the time of writing) a
director of the Body Shop International, and one of
many workaholic husband-and-wife teams who
flourish in the caring, creative company run by that
high-profile work enthusiast Anita Roddick and her
husband, Gordon.

Forster for many years ran her own company,
which handled the Body Shop's publicity. Naturally,
some of this involved leaving her family in order to
follow Roddick around the world. When she had the
choice of getting her hair done for her wedding or
finishing an important PR project, for a workaholic
like Forster there was little doubt about what to do –
and her husband-to-be supported her decision – so she
went to her wedding with her beautiful red hair
unadorned. Lamond, who worked for the Bank of
England at the time, knew what he was letting himself
in for when he married Forster, she says, 'because he
had already been coerced into dressing up as Action
Man to help me promote Palitoy'.

She is delighted that they are now working together
so that 'we can talk about work together all the time'.
They have two children, who are looked after by a
full-time nanny, and harbour little guilt about that. 'I
was quite pressurized by my family, all of whom are
either doctors or judges,' Forster remembers, 'and I
was determined that my children would not be.' She
takes pleasure in recalling how she signed the
contracts to begin her own business just a day after
her younger son was born.

As for Anita Roddick herself, she is well known for
spending her 'holidays' travelling around the world in
search of exotic facial scrubs and rare natural

ingredients – such as nightingale droppings – for her Body Shop potions. She is continually looking for new products and ways of helping Third World people to become more profitably productive, and jokes: 'There's usually only something furry in the fridge, but Gordon doesn't seem to mind.' When she speaks of her work, she lights up with an enthusiasm that is more beautifying than any Body Shop cosmetic.

It's when one partner is obsessive about work and the other can't comprehend the attraction that marriages and families break up. After all, there's nothing wrong if talking about net turnover and gross national products turns you *both* on – it's probably more productive than just talking 'dirty'. But when one partner feels an unwelcome third in the bed, or starts using 'work' as an end to justify all meanness – that's when the trouble starts. These people may then need a type of help that goes well beyond the realms of this book.

Workaholism seems to work best in couples if both partners have it in equal degrees and are, as some experts call it, 'in phase': like the contemporary Renaissance man Gyles Brandreth and his wife, the author and historian Michele Brown, whose fingers are interlocked in so many professional pies that they claim to have board meetings, for maximum efficiency, while brushing their teeth.

But it can be a relief for a workaholic to live alone, as personnel director Paula Grayson has discovered. Grayson, like Forster, a thirty-something raised with a powerful work ethic, likes to think of herself as a 'workafrolic' – someone who works hard and plays hard too. And since she interjects an element of fun into her work, she also sees nothing wrong in mixing business with pleasure since business *is* a pleasure to her. Personnel director for Luton College of Higher Education, chairman of the recruitment working party of the Institute of Personnel Management and with numerous other subsidiary titles – 'the sure sign of a workaholic,' she chuckles – she takes her work along with her on holidays, whipping out her briefcase for secret sessions whenever the need arises.

The group of friends with whom she regularly shares canal-boat holidays have threatened to throw her work into the river, so she has become more cunning about deceiving them – for their peace of mind, she rationalizes, more than her own. But why should friends feel the holiday is threatened if she takes out a stack of papers to peruse in a leisurely fashion instead of the latest trashy novel?

'People who live with a workaholic seem to get cross with you for your own sake usually, not theirs,' she says charitably. They don't understand that for the workaholic, to whom work is a perpetual holiday because they derive such pleasure from it, holidays that require a complete switch-off feel more like exile!

Grayson gives the impression of being tremendously organized and efficient, but maintains she is a 'deadline workaholic' whose mind is crystallized by the immediacy of deadlines and who often prepares her best speeches the night before. One reason why 'deadline workaholics' are attracted to particular jobs is that they give them the stimulus they require. Those whose jobs don't provide precise enough deadlines are often disciplined enough to impose their own. It is when they begin to create imaginary ones, like 'I *must* get this report on widgets done over the weekend', and make their loved ones' lives hell in the process over a paper no one really wants to see anyway, that they are in trouble. Or when they begin to crave deadlines to such a degree that unless the adrenaline is flowing full-speed they can't even psych themselves up to sharpen a pencil!

Although she is involved in a long-standing romantic relationship, her (also workaholic) partner lives abroad for much of the year, and Grayson admits that the solitude this imposes on her can be a relief at times: they can each pursue their work wholeheartedly and enjoy each other wholeheartedly when they are together. She considers it a luxury to be able to work deep into the night without worrying about offending anyone, and to be able to do her vacuuming at midnight, when she's run out of mental steam for more demanding tasks.

She insists she's never experienced the downside of workaholism – 'the sense that everything is getting on top of you' – but then, she always tries to take a lunch break, she says, 'and finds time to talk to people. That's very important.'

Heather Tilbury's husband of seventeen years, Donald Phillips, is a placid, good-natured Michelin man (he works for the tyre company) to whom workaholism is anathema but who understands and supports his wife's addiction to her work. Tilbury, who regularly works twelve-hour days running her own public relations company, says, 'I originally trained as a dancer and put all the energy and drive of my ballet into my business. I thought, at first, that I'd spend two days a week on it and dance the rest of the time, but it completely took over!' Her husband accepts that, 'Any plans we have go by the board. There's never any way we can say what we're going to do on Thursday night because the chances are Heather will have to be working. And she can't bear to see me sitting down and doing nothing because she's always doing something, even when she sits down. I've learned to cook pretty well, but the one thing I do insist on is that we take holidays out of the country, where it's difficult for her to reach or be reached by the office.'

'I still manage to call the office, even from Greece and Turkey,' Tilbury chimes in. 'I sometimes pretend I'm going shopping and give them a ring.' She was such a workaholic, she boasts, that when she was handling the Lycra account and spotted a Lycra dress in a Greek boutique, she had to stop the boat and get off to see how it was selling. The Phillipses have a weekend home in the country, but she inevitably brings work along with her there.

The female workaholic, as Mr Phillips points out, is a fairly recent phenomenon. She was celebrated – or condemned – in a succession of 1980s films such as *Broadcast News*, *Baby Boom* and *Working Girl* – and we will look at her particular problems in greater detail in a later chapter. Suffice it to say that many's the time I've been writing a feature on divorce with my husband threatening it if he doesn't get his dinner before midnight, and a fellow female freelance once confided how her own baby was screaming for her attention in the bedroom while she was hurriedly penning a piece on the National Society for the Prevention of Cruelty to Children – pausing only long enough to note the irony.

Well-known female workaholics include Elizabeth Esteve-Coll, director of the Victoria and Albert Museum, a widow who once admitted that her life revolves largely around the museum and that she takes 'sacks full' of papers home with her; television exercise expert Lizzie Webb, who says she gets a 'buzz' from exercising her abilities almost around the clock; and television presenter Esther Rantzen, married to the equally hard-working producer Desmond Wilcox, who continued working even through two bouts of pneumonia, collapsing at one point in 1989 and publicly promising to 'take things easier for the sake of the family'. (But shortly afterwards she was quoted as saying that she was afraid her public would forget her if she were not seen as frequently on television.)

Since society is less accommodating to female workaholics, they are often single or divorced if they have not managed to involve their partners in their work – as Leah Hertz observed in her seminal study of top female entrepreneurs of the 1980s, *The Business Amazons* (André Deutsch, 1986). And since women are generally more accommodating than men and more anxious to prove themselves in a man's world, they are predisposed to becoming reluctant workaholics out of a desire to please workaholic bosses or to conform to the demands of a workaholic corporate culture.

At the London Secretary Show at Olympia in 1990, secretaries were warned that they were as or *more* likely to find themselves under stress than their bosses. 'The problem with being a secretary is that the job is not well defined,' said the stress-management therapist Patricia Hodgkins at the time. 'The boss will often expect you to be a marriage-guidance counsellor, remember his wife's birthday and organize theatre tickets, as well as doing all the typing and office work.' She advised them on the importance of learning how to say 'no' – a word many workaholics have difficulty in forming.

The workaholic boss need not be a nightmare if he or she is aware that subordinates do not necessarily share their undying dedication to the job. As Heather Tilbury says, 'I bully my staff to go home by 6 pm even though I usually stay on until about 7.30 or 8 pm myself. I live above the shop and have to stop myself from staying on and on, and I'm usually in by 8 am – but I'd never expect my staff to keep the same hours as I do.' But Tilbury confesses to a workaholic inclination to involve herself in accounts she has turned over to employees in a manner she acknowledges may irritate her highly responsible staff just a teensy-weensy bit.

The workaholic employee who smugly munches sandwiches at the desk instead of going out to chew the fat with colleagues, who arrives hours earlier than necessary and strikes up more than a nodding acquaintance with the late-night cleaners, may be even more widely disliked than the workaholic boss. He or she can be seen as letting the side down, 'teacher's pet', an ingratiating wimp or a serious subversive.

And whereas the boss's belief that his or her work is terribly important may be justified to some degree if it actually *is* (and delusions of indispensability may have some small basis in fact), the workaholic 'drone' is more likely to be using his or her workaholism to cloak other insecurities. As Professor Janet Spence notes, 'Work enthusiasts are usually white-collar workers in interesting and influential jobs. Blue-collar workers or those in routine jobs tend to channel their energies into hobbies and other activities – or to be workaholic in a much more *driven*, less constructive, way.' Like the spinster clerk in Bernice Rubens' novel *A Five Year Sentence* (W H Allen, 1978) who had used the monotonous routine of her work to fill the emptiness of her personal life, and determined to kill herself on her enforced retirement, only to be kept alive unwillingly by the perspicacious parting present of a five-year diary which – to her meticulous mind – demanded to be filled.

Certain professions, such as medicine and politics, demand a workaholic dedication, and those who balk at working inhuman hours should probably not consider such vocations – despite encouraging recent campaigns to make the hours in both these professions more human. Houseman Chris Johnstone made history by seeking an injunction forbidding Blooms-bury Health Authority to force him to work more than seventy-two hours a week – still arguably too much for the health of either the doctor or the patients. He was hailed as a hero by some and decried as a traitor by others, particularly those who had already managed to survive the system and didn't see why it should be made easier for their successors.

The famous heart-transplant surgeon Magdi Yacoub – like other great medical men – has been praised for his ability to work almost around the clock and credited with superhuman stamina by those who have worked with him. 'What happens if Mr Yacoub's ever sick when a heart becomes available?' I once naïvely inquired. 'Mr Yacoub's never sick,' was the unequivocal reply. It must be difficult for such celebrated workaholics not to push themselves ever harder in order to live up to their own legend.

Psychiatrist Dr Desmond Kelly, an internationally recognized stress expert, says that medicine – like journalism, the law and other obviously high-pressure professions – attract Type A personalities with a tendency towards workaholism in the first place. 'They're demanding, exacting and addictive,' says Kelly, 'although the health service has many workaholics who are motivated by idealism – like Magdi Yacoub, who is a medical saint and a true workaholic in the best sense.'

It is intriguing to note that most of the specialists on workaholism and occupational stress demonstrate, even before they eventually confess it, that they themselves are workaholic. Dr Kelly freely admits that he is: 'I work on Saturdays to shift the paper which I don't have time for during the week,' he says apologetically, and the string of titles he carries – President of the International Stress Management Association, Medical Director of the Priory Hospital, London, Chairman of the Priory Hospitals Group – in addition to his own practice are a dead giveaway.

Hugh Jenkins, director of the Institute of Family Therapy, which deals with many families devastated by the effects of the worst kinds of workaholism, says, 'I often wonder how we are to help others when we put ourselves through such hoops. There is inevitably a real tension between caring for others and caring for yourself.' He had just come back from his first real holiday in years, in which he became 'reacquainted' with his wife and four children and found it 'wonderfully refreshing to read novels instead of papers for work'. But he was generally unrepentant about his workaholism, although he felt his children's childhood was 'flashing by too quickly' and agreed that his wife, 'who works but is not a workaholic', might voice a different opinion.

Dr Malcolm Carruthers and his wife, the psychotherapist Vera Diamond, spend a considerable part of their professional lives dealing with the after-effects of burnout caused by overwork and lack of play. Yet they are both unabashed workaholics. 'The workaholic is a very misunderstood person,' says Carruthers, who can stay up until the wee hours, oblivious to the time, happily tinkering with his computerized system for monitoring stress and job satisfaction, using what he calls 'chemo-feedback'.

At his Harley Street Positive Health Clinic (and the several other anti-stress and hormone-replacement-therapy clinics for men and women which he runs from the same address) he keeps all sorts of sophisticated equipment for measuring stress levels and calculating whether patients are set on a self-destruct course. Diamond once threatened to divorce him, 'naming his computer and all of his committees as co-respondents'.

'But if it's one of her patients in a psychotherapeutic crisis and they have to stay up talking until three or four in the morning, that's different,' he teases. Fortunately, they are both what Carruthers calls 'well-adapted' workaholics, who have adjusted to each other's work habits and work well together, and often late into the night, as they create stress-management programmes for industry.

Admittedly, the meditation and autogenic training – a form of relaxation therapy – they both teach has helped them to adapt and survive their workaholic life style. But both think it would be more difficult to be married to someone who wasn't a workaholic.

Dr John Nicholson, executive chairman of the leading human resources consultancy, John Nicholson Associates, and the business psychologist involved with British Telecom's workaholic advertisements, produced a special self-analysis booklet to be sent out to all the worried executives who wrote in for BT's 'Workplan' in response to the campaign. This attempted to ascertain whether respondents missed family occasions because of work, stayed late at the office, brought work home and even dreamed about work problems – the implication of the latter being, of course, that better telecommunications could solve most of their problems.

He discovered that more than three-quarters of his respondents felt they worked too hard, and that more than half put in at least a ten-hour day. Almost the same number took every opportunity to work – even going home on the train – and that they cancelled family holidays and forgot their children's birthdays. Eight out of ten of the 102 men and thirty-eight women executives who filled in his questionnaire (or got someone else to fill it in for them) blamed marital rows and the loss of friendship on their dedication to duty.

Yet even Nicholson admits it too: 'Of course I'm a workaholic! If you're lucky enough to be doing a job you really love, of course you are. I own my own company and it's very difficult to have a reason to stop.'

An academic psychologist when he first joined Jaguar in the early 1980s, he has since become one of Britain's top corporate counsellors, teaching people that 'working smarter' doesn't necessarily mean working harder, and that 'It is impossible to motivate anyone: you've got to create a climate in which they motivate themselves.'

According to American corporate consultant William Bridges, quoted in *Fortune* magazine in 1990, '"work smarter" is usually a euphemism for "work harder next week"'.

Professor Cary Cooper, author of numerous books on stress and creator of the occupational stress tables for the *Sunday Times*, also cheerfully confesses he's a workaholic. Like Nicholson, Kelly and Carruthers, his professional output is astounding, and he comes to each new task with apparently renewed zest. His wife Rachel Cooper, a lecturer who co-authored *Living with Stress* (Penguin, 1988) with him is resigned to the fact that 'His holidays are always combined with conferences or giving papers somewhere.'

Yet Cooper, a Californian, is careful to schedule some special time with Rachel and their young children. It is a second marriage for each of them, so they are particularly conscious of the need to make time for themselves as a couple. 'Wednesday nights are our nights,' Professor Cooper explained on the publication of his book *Career Couples* (Unwin Hyman, 1989). 'We go swimming and talk, and this is a conscious "coping strategy" of the kind recommended in the book.' These 'coping strategies' – which successful workaholics have usually already worked out, albeit subconsciously – are crucial, Professor Cooper feels, to remaining well balanced.

Sir John Harvey-Jones, for example, the former ICI chairman who now runs his own consultancy and acts as a business 'troubleshooter', finds that a clear division between work and leisure is important to him. He may work between 7 am and 10 pm every weekday, but, as he once told the *Sunday Times*, 'I have never worked at home, holidays have always been sacrosanct and I protect my weekends with the fire of a mother lion.'

The workaholic 'foodie' and restaurateur Prudence Leith – winner of the Veuve Cliquot Businesswoman of the Year award in 1991 – is totally dedicated to her work and adores it. But she keeps a hideaway home in the Cotswolds, is guarded by a redoubtable 'dragon' of a secretary-cum-personal assistant, who protects her from unwelcome, time-wasting approaches and has limited her sixteen-hour days now to the middle of the week – with 'very big chunks off' for relaxation and recuperation, and plenty of holiday time with her family.

Elizabeth Dole, US Secretary of Transportation under Ronald Reagan, Secretary of Labor under George Bush and at the time of writing President of the American Red Cross, was a workaholic long before she married the workaholic presidential aspirant Senator Bob Dole. When I visited her in Washington,

DC, she told me that she thought she and her husband kept sane despite their punishing schedules, 'because we try to keep Sundays special – as church and family time'. And she was confident enough in her abilities to know that she could resign her Secretary's post to support her husband's campaign without any long-term damage to her own career.

Well-balanced workaholics will have worked out subtle ways of minimizing stress for themselves and those around them – a subject which will be expanded upon in later chapters – so that to the rest of the world they may seem magically capable of withstanding almost superhuman stresses. And since in the 1980s stress became imbued with super-star status, so in one sense did the workaholic. It was fashionable to boast about how many hours you spent at your desk, 'breakfast' meetings – an idea that caught on from America – made work a movable feast in which it was 'wimpish' *not* to participate and the concept of 'corporate hospitality' – another American import – expanded to encroach on the evenings and weekends of senior managers and their families.

British executives used to recount with amazement, and some amusement, how their American counterparts would entertain them, take them out to dinner and even invite them to their homes at weekends when they went to do business in the States. In the 1980s they found themselves expected to do the same thing. And concurrent with the trend towards assertiveness and management training to encourage women into business was one in coaching courses for the 'corporate wife' (another American concept), who was required to make such entertaining go smoothly. Wendy Walden, who ran an 'executive wives' programme, would even research husbands' companies for these wives, so that they could converse intelligently about them! Many wives became resentful about how their husbands' work would expand to fill *their* time.

Dual-career couples supported a burgeoning business in 'personal service' industries – personal services provided by a new generation of shrewd young entrepreneurs such as Sophy Morgan-Jones, daughter of Jennifer d'Abo, whose Short Cut company typified those which would not only clean your house, water your plants and walk your dog but also organize a complete removal, choose the right plants to complement the house they had arranged to have decorated for you and pick the right dog for your requirements. In 1990 *The Times* began to run a regular weekly feature highlighting just such services – for people to whom time was more precious than money, and who didn't mind working to pay the party arranger and the personal shopper, as well as the nanny, gardener and cleaning service their workaholic lifestyle required. If some – even those in exalted positions – had stopped long enough to add up the cost of all these support services, they might have discovered they would have been financially better off *not* working. But that would not have deterred the true workaholic!

Catalogue companies, originally catering to rural recluses, housebound housewives or those who appreciated the opportunity to spread payments over a long period, furiously worked on their image and relaunched themselves as the executive woman's friend. With twenty-four hour ordering and the promise of forty-eight-hours courier delivery (an idea pioneered by George Davies with his mould-breaking Next Directory), power suits, silk underwear and leather briefcases pushed the traditional flowery frocks and sturdy girdles to the back pages.

While companies invested in often mandatory 'motivational' breaks as never before ('motivation' was another new boom industry in the 1980s), which could involve employees in survival courses with ex-SAS commandos or war games with spray paints in an effort to imbue them with greater enthusiasm for the job, British executives became increasingly loath to take up their full holiday entitlement – another transatlantic trend. 'In Washington,' wrote Michael Kinsley in *Time* magazine in August 1990, 'the easiest way to flatter someone is to say, "You must be very busy." (And the most disconcerting answer is, "No, not really.") It is today's ritualistic form of obeisance. It means, "You must be very important."'

Professor Cooper confirmed: 'There was a feeling that high-stress jobs were good because they made people important. And we all want to feel important.' He was amazed, he says, 'by the way when I did my occupational stress tables a few years ago for the *Sunday Times* I got letters from irate librarians and museum-keepers furious at being at the bottom of the stress list. They should have been *happy*!'

Kinsley wittily challenged the workaholic ethic, which, he felt, was making Americans get their priorities in a twist. Headlined 'You must be very busy', his essay attacked the American attitude to holidays – which he called 'chintzy' compared with that of other nations. The British, he claimed, 'on average work thirty-nine hours a week, get eight paid holidays and enjoy twenty-five days – five weeks – of

paid vacation a year', the Germans a thirty-eight-hour
week with ten holidays and six weeks of paid leave, as
compared with 'maybe three if we're lucky' for
Americans.

He went on to speculate that, 'The equation of
busy-ness with importance may help to explain
Americans' queasiness about vacations', and cited the
following example. 'The *Washington Post* reports that
two days before Iraq invaded Kuwait, when troops
were already massed on the border, someone tried to
reach the head of Kuwait's civil defence, only to be
told he was on vacation for the next three weeks. Go
ahead and laugh. But is that any more absurd than
American TV news anchor Dan Rather, who was on
vacation in France, spending the day of the invasion
desperately scouring the Middle East for a place to
broadcast from and ultimately settling on London –
rather than permitting a war to occur while he was
off-duty?'

It depends upon your (workaholic or not) perspective.
A true work enthusiast would understand the fury
and frustration the high-profile newsman Rather
must have experienced on being on holiday when
what might have been the story of a lifetime broke. It
must have been closely akin to the feelings of the
Tornado pilot confined to hospital when he longed to
be at the front line, and the sentiments of the German
correspondent for a British publication who was
apparently on holiday when the Berlin Wall fell.

The upper echelons of the working world are
probably pretty evenly divided between those to
whom holidays are sacrosanct and those who would
sacrifice them at a second's notice to cope with a
company crisis or to further their career. Some are

simply opportunists; others have identified so strongly with their job that, as for Dan Rather, it would be torture to endure enforced idleness when events that could have profound professional repercussions were taking place.

Some chief executives – like the senior civil servants I have occasionally had the misfortune to try and contact over the Christmas holidays – leave strict orders that they are never to be disturbed. Others insist that if anything at all untoward should occur, they wish to know about it, others again phone their offices so regularly that, as far as their partners, children and secretaries are concerned, they might as well not be away.

Kinsley opines: 'One of the most admirable things about Ronald Reagan as President was his freedom from time snobbery. There was a man who didn't worry that his importance was measured by the number of hours or days he spent at his desk. George Bush seems to have inherited the same healthy attitude.'

Healthy it may be to put up a 'Gone fishing' sign on the door of the Oval Office when an international incident erupts, but was it what the people (particularly of such a workaholic nation) expected of their president when the Gulf crisis started? There was a mixed reaction form the American media at the time, with some praising President Bush for his independent spirit and unwillingness to give the appearance of having been 'held hostage in the White House'. But some of the relatives of the real hostages held in Kuwait spoke bitterly of what they saw as the President's lack of respect for the situation. 'We don't mind that he's having a holiday,' someone said, 'but you'd think he could at least put on a suit and tie when he gives his television interviews.'

Something about the smiling, wind-swept President pictured playing on his boat while young reservists were being tearfully wrested from their families was disturbing – no matter how beneficial it may have been for the President's own psyche. And even though, thanks to the wonders of modern technology, he could (theoretically) keep his finger on the 'button' as easily on his boat as in his office, many felt he had lost touch with the pulse of the nation.

The late, great foreign correspondent David Blundy (like Dan Rather, Kate Adie and others of that ilk – irrespressibly workaholic) painted an amusing picture of the difficulty in contacting the President 'buffeting around in a power boat off the coast of Maine' as important news broke. Blundy observed: 'President Bush is on holiday and is distinctly less interested in affairs of state than in getting his body in shape. Mr Bush takes "fun stuff", as he calls it, very seriously indeed. He was asked about Poland as he played golf next morning and said: "No comment". Asked about his holiday, the President said, "Now you're talking."'

There were many *thankful* reports at the time, however, that Vice-President Dan Quayle remained on holiday for so long. *Newsweek* magazine asked the question, 'Should Quayle just stay in Arizona?', which the *Washington Post* columnist Richard Cohen answered with a resounding, 'Yes.'

It was the British cabinet, under their workaholic Prime Minister Margaret Thatcher, who cut short their holidays while the American President was photographed whooping it up in Kennebunkport – substantially weakening Kinsley's theory. *The Times* reported, on 11 August 1990, that, 'Unlike President Bush, who has decamped from Washington for his annual holiday, senior British ministers have had to put their personal travel agendas on hold because of events in the Middle East. Mrs Thatcher's assembly of a Falklands-style inner cabinet has torpedoed the holiday plans of her most senior ministers.'

The Opposition leader Neil Kinnock, however, according to *The Times*, was 'keeping abreast of the crisis via Italian radio and television. He is sunning himself in Tuscany.' Clearly he didn't remember the frosty reception his predecessor Jim Callaghan received in 1979, when he returned from the Caribbean with the attitude 'Crisis? What crisis?' to a Britain 'shuddered to a freezing, strike-bound halt', as the *Daily Telegraph* put it at the time. The former model Twiggy summed up the feeling of a large part of the country when she was quoted in the *Daily Mail* as saying, 'How dare a Prime Minister fly home and say he has been lounging about in a luxury swimming pool and there's nothing to worry about? We may as well give Margaret Thatcher a chance. No one could be worse than Jim Callaghan.'

A good leader, most people believe, is one who gives at least the appearance of being willing to go down with the ship, and though companies now worry about the health of employees who do *not* take their full holiday entitlement, according to Dr Kelly, they still tend to expect that sort of diehard dedication from those at the top – a conflicting message which can lead to more stress among those who have not charted their own, coping, compromise course.

Some companies, such as the London management consultants Coopers & Lybrand Deloitte, say they are now monitoring and enforcing holiday entitlements. 'This is not altruistic,' the personnel director David Seddon told the *Sunday Times*. 'The company wants to encourage balanced employees because they are more productive. It is for completely mercenary reasons.' A four-year study by Aston University Business School of 700 people with jobs demanding a lot of driving concluded early in 1991 that middle-aged drivers were much less stressed on Mondays and Fridays, because they had just enjoyed or were anticipating relaxing weekends, whereas younger drivers, who had more frenetically social weekends, were least stressed in the middle of the week and were the most prone to tension and frustration generally.

A survey in *Personnel Today* magazine in 1990 revealed that workaholic senior executives were causing concern among some personnel managers by their refusal to go on holiday, and that there was considerable confusion among personnel experts on how damaging this might be, and how much benefit holidays were. While nearly all questioned said they thought people performed better with regular time off, over half said they thought one week away was as refreshing as two. Yet according to Dr Andrew Meluish, medical adviser to Henley Management College, quoted in *The Times* at around the same time as the piece in *Personnel Today*, a *three*-week break was considered ideal, because 'it takes two or three days to wind down on holiday, to get the adrenaline of work out of your system. It takes another one or two days to build back to returning to work.'

Many workaholics actually become sick during their holidays, just as work ambivalents become sick in order to obtain an unofficial holiday. Dr Vernon

Coleman, author of the books *Bodypower* (Thames & Hudson, 1983), *Mindpower* (Thames & Hudson, 1984) and *Toxic Stress* (Chilton Designs, 1991), talks of the 'bargain' he made with his body to stay well until he finished a book tour and *then* to resume the streaming cold from which he was suffering. We all make similar 'bargains', he believes – consciously or unconsciously – with ourselves.

One conscientious worker, who wouldn't call herself a workaholic, found that she invariably became ill on holiday, having held up under the strain of a demanding ten-hours-a-day job for months in between. 'This time it was septicaemia as well as the flu,' she mournfully confided to me after her holiday. 'But at least I had them in Barbados!'

To other workaholics holidays are a vital tonic, whether they involve elements of work (like the international conference capers chronicled in David Lodge's novel *Small World*) or provide a counterpoint to it.

Entrepreneur Richard Branson (whose business is other people's holidays and leisure interests) has called Virgin Airlines the first love of his life. But he manages to make plenty of time for the other loves in his life (his family, his sports and his ambitious aerial endeavours) and says he keeps holidays 'sacrosanct'.

Former Sock Shop supremo, Sophie Mirman, and her husband and business partner, Richard Ross, who bounced back after their multimillion-pound empire crumpled, to run a children's shop in Chelsea, feel that 'long weekends are as good as expensive holidays'.

Anita and Gordon Roddick often holiday with friends who happen to be involved, like so many of the people they know, in their business. The make-up

artist Barbara Daly – creator of the Colourings range
of cosmetics for the Body Shop – and her husband,
Laurence Tarlo, who works with her, are among their
favourite holiday companions, and they like adven-
turous ones, such as safaris. The Colourings range
was dreamed up, Daly once told me, during a
brainstorming session on a communal holiday with
the Roddicks.

Most successful work enthusiasts have worked out
their own, individual, holiday philosophy.

The *Personnel Today* survey showed that only 22 per
cent of managerial staff routinely took their full
average holiday entitlement of 25.5 days a year, as
compared with four out of five *non*-managers taking
their full average entitlement of 24.3 days.

But at least those at the top usually exert
considerable control over their work, and with the
sense of responsibility that causes them to cut short or
cancel holidays there is likely to come a sense of
reward from the work which can seem, to the true
work enthusiast, as refreshing as a holiday. 'A sense of
control is crucial,' says Professor Cooper, who
personally plumps for holidays of the busman's
variety more often than not. 'Being a secretary can be
more stressful than being the boss.' But then, so much
in life is a matter of perception, and those who
perceive themselves to be in control of their work, at
whatever level, are much more likely to thrive on it.
Workaholics whose work is controlling *them* need not
just a holiday but a permanent new perspective.

3

Working Less, Enjoying It More?

The people mentioned in the previous chapter are, for the most part, quite extraordinary achievers. But we are all familiar with the adage that work expands to fill the time allotted to it, and know from our own experience that this is so.

Productivity is no sure measure of a workaholic. Someone who gives the appearance of constant activity may be doing little more than chasing their own tail, whereas someone who takes long holidays, gives personal life a high priority and leaves plenty of time to just sit – as well as just sitting and thinking – can be more productive in the long run. A 'leisure intelligence report' by Mintel, the market research agency, at the beginning of 1991 revealed that 'a staggering 70 per cent of the population spend a substantial part of their leisure time doing absolutely nothing', and finds that 'literally just sitting and relaxing or daydreaming is one of the most popular pastimes'!

You can run round as frantically as the White Rabbit in *Alice in Wonderland* and not be a workaholic, or be a workaholic who still takes plenty of time to sit and think. Even so, more workaholics – generally time-urgent Type As (A for aggressive adrenaline addicts) – hare around frantically than plod methodically on with the job, like benign Type Bs. Think of the tortoise and hare, and how the tortoise often ends up ahead.

Grace Sheppard, wife of the high-profile Bishop of Liverpool confided to me that she thought 'people sometimes resent the fact that David is such an *achieving* sort of person when he takes so much time off. But there's no point in him recommending that his clergy take time to renew themselves unless he does it himself!' The Sheppards unashamedly schedule generous holiday time at the beginning of every year, and fit in working engagements around it. And both manage to publish, broadcast and paint, in addition to a rigorous round of pastoral duties.

The management consultant John Nicholson is daring enough to suggest that, 'We may have become workaholics in Britain because we are incompetent. The British disease is no longer strikes; it is lack of training compared with other European nations.' Professor Cary Cooper agrees. 'In a study we did on European chief executive officers [CEOs], we found that the majority of them worked either "always" or "frequently" over the weekend – except for the Germans. They worked *less* than anybody else at the weekend, had the most outside interests and yet their country was the most efficient! If a CEO is a good time-manager and priority-setter, he should be able to manage perfectly well during a five-day week, and be brave enough to say, "I can't function on less than six

hours' sleep a night – and I need time with my family."
In the long run he'll be more effective.' Cooper's
research indicates that after forty-five hours a week,
work is likely to become 25 per cent less productive –
and that when somebody works between sixty and
eighty hours a week they are putting their health at
risk – although, of course, this depends on how they
work and what their 'coping strategies' are. Yet the
research of 'priority management' proponent Dan
Stamp, for his report on The 21st Century Workplace
(published in 1990), after surveying 1,300 business
people in eight countries, showed that 'the average
business person has thirty-six hours of work on his
desk at any one time' and that '95 per cent of business
people regularly work in excess of a standard work
week.'

Crispin Tweddell, CEO of the Piper Trust, an
innovative retail consultancy in London which advises
many major companies, says he's not impressed by
employees who arrive early and leave late and seem
terribly busy at their desks in between. 'People who
are too "busy" never get enough time for quality
thinking,' Tweddell cautions his clients. 'If they are
tearing from meeting to meeting and have to make
decisions, they're not necessarily quality decisions.'
Sometimes, he suspects, people may be piling their
desks with papers and filling their appointment books
because they are afraid to be alone with their thoughts
– whatever their quality.

Professor Cooper also warns against the 'full
briefcase syndrome', in which workaholics carry a full
case of work home with them every night to fall asleep
over. He's been guilty of it himself, he says. 'It's very
important to assess results: being frantically busy

without being productive can mean a workaholic is actually hiding – from himself.'

The estate agent Jan Morgan, who founded and runs Grosvenor International, a company dealing in prime properties at prime prices, is normally a highly efficient work enthusiast. But she once told me (for a *Sunday Express Magazine* feature I was doing on how divorce could affect the health) how, during an unhappy period in her life, she suddenly found herself working more frantically than ever before. 'I would come to the office early and stay until late and delude myself that I was getting a great deal done – until I looked at the figures and realized that they had been lower than ever before during that period!'

Margaret Thatcher, one of the most notable workaholics in British public life this century, whose puritan work ethic shaped the era that was named for her, was said to have prided herself that she knew as much about each government department as any of the ministers responsible for them.

'There's nothing admirable in duplicating all that effort,' says Dr Nicholson. 'She had no *right* to be so well informed, and plenty of company chairmen and managing directors make the same mistake. It's a stupid thing to do! A senior manager should be bold and confident enough to select a team of really good people and leave them to get on with the job, so that the top person becomes a sort of philosopher-king less concerned with detail and more with thinking and strategic planning.'

Another potentially undermining workaholic syndrome was eventually the cause of Margaret Thatcher's undoing. She certainly didn't suffer from the 'tortoise and the hare' syndrome, but was a prime proponent of what I think of as the 'queen bee' syndrome – which can, in the long run, prove equally destructive.

This is a syndrome in which workaholics are spurred on by success, so that they become as dependent as an addict upon the power and glory their efforts have brought them and eventually come to completely define themselves by their position – as anyone who saw Mrs Thatcher pathetically reiterating her intention to go 'on and on' would suspect she had done.

It was clear that Mrs Thatcher had stopped defining herself merely as a politician. She identified herself totally as *the* Prime Minister, and for her there was never to be any alternative, no U-turn was ever conceivable. Her famous 'We are a grandmother' gaffe demonstrated the delusions of grandeur from which such queen bees often suffer. For such workaholics the very thought of retirement, or of stepping back and letting someone else make the running, is anathema. They must always be at the centre of the hive of activity.

It is particularly appropriate to call it the 'queen bee' syndrome because it is one which, alas, all too frequently afflicts those rare women who have managed – inevitably by almost superhuman efforts – to make their way to the top. The chair of the Equal Opportunities Commission, Joanna Foster (a workaholic of a very different kind), thinks of a queen bee as the kind of woman who wants to keep all the honey for herself.

Like Queen Elizabeth I (to whom her devoted admirer Lord Hailsham once likened her) and other queen bees, Mrs Thatcher chose to surround herself with dutiful male drones who would never outshine her.

I knew an ageing editor who was similarly afflicted, regarding every up-and-coming writer as a threat to her pre-eminence, and instead of winning their loyalty by acting as a mentor, she never allowed a successor to be trained to fill her shoes. She worked almost frantically, as if out of panic that she would someday be supplanted and lose, together with her supremacy in the workplace, her own sense of self-worth. For a compulsively *driven* workaholic – as opposed to a bright-eyed 'work enthusiast' – needs to reassure herself perpetually of her own indispensability.

While it is understandable if someone considers themselves indispensable to their own business, few employees – however highly paid and regarded – cannot be dispensed with, as the workaholic George Davies of Next discovered to his dismay and to the shock of the nation, which had taken him to its heart as an entrepreneur in corporate clothing.

The 'men in grey suits' put paid to Davies as surely as they did to Margaret Thatcher and, in a fashion, to Sir John Egan (at the time of writing, chief executive of the British Aviation Authority), who gracefully bowed out of Jaguar when it was taken over by Ford, and others who, largely because of their work-enthusiast's qualities, had a vision and a sense of vocation for their job. Which meant that as the 1980s drew to a close, so to a large degree did the era of charismatic, workaholic leaders – for better or for worse.

After eleven and a half years under a workaholic leader renowned for her ability to exist on four hours' sleep a night (supplemented with Churchillian cat-naps) and for her avowed intention to go 'on and on', 'UK plc' found itself at the true dawn of the 1990s with a chief executive who was a proponent of a much more nine-to-five approach and sounded – from the moment he took office – as if he was looking forward to an early retirement.

Barely had Margaret Thatcher left Downing Street, dazedly muttering 'We have always worked – it's the only thing we know', than her successor and his wife were indicating that they intended to treat what she had regarded as a vocation as a day-job which would not intrude unduly into out-of-work hours. Mrs Major insisted on remaining at the family home in Huntingdon with her two teenage children rather than moving above the shop, as is expected of a prime ministerial spouse, and Mr Major's tacit support of her decision demonstrated that he condoned the concept of drawing a tangible line of demarcation between professional duties and private life. (This was not an attitude that had found much favour in Thatcher's Britain, where lunch was for wimps and only 'wets' went home to dinner on time.)

In a television interview early in December 1990 John Major made it clear that he 'had a life before politics' and intended 'to have a life after politics' – as well as maintaining his interests outside it, like watching Surrey play cricket and Chelsea play football and enjoying opera with his wife Norma. He stressed his outside interests in successive interviews, making it clear (through protesting – too much?) that he had no intention of becoming a slave to the job.

The Majors' seemingly offhand attitude towards the highest office in the land affronted some and was applauded by others. Observers were divided between those who said 'Good for them!' and wanted (like the Liberal Democrat leader Paddy Ashdown and the Labour MP Harriet Harman) to go even further towards making a parliamentary career compatible with home life, and those who regarded the Majors' desire to retain a suburban semi-detachment from the top job in the land as an affront to the dignity of the premiership.

In their quiet way the Majors were daringly iconoclastic, shattering the myth of the divine right of absolute dedication which dogged so many ambitious aspirants during the Thatcher years. Despite Mr Major's remark that, 'If you haven't done an hour and a half's work before 7.30 am and then gone into a transport café for breakfast, I promise you haven't lived' – the Majors seemed to be suggesting, in their unassuming way, that it was possible to be Prime Minister perfectly efficiently from nine-ish to five-ish, Monday to Friday, and Mr and Mrs Average at evenings and weekends.

'I hope they succeed,' Professor Cooper admitted to me early in the Major administration. 'Differentiating between personal and professional roles is very healthy. John Major, like the CEOs we studied, is in his forties, and this could make a big difference to attitudes towards work in the future. Forty-year-olds have younger families and want to spend more time with them than their predecessors who set the pace in their fifties and sixties. That's going to make them saner in the long run. They have seen too many older colleagues burnt out or getting heart attacks, and they have a healthier attitude to work which is going to make their companies healthier. Maybe they know they are going to be at the top for longer – and they see the need to pace themselves.'

The new attitude awakening among chief executives of the 'baby-boom' generation in both Britain and America is being met with a rush of similar sentiment from their junior colleagues, the twenty-somethings *Fortune* magazine dubbed the 'baby-busters', who 'are nothing at all like the workaholic yuppies who preceded them'.

Baby-busters or 'yiffies', as the magazine called them – for 'young, individualistic, freedom-minded and few' – are 'the employees who can afford to say no,' because the job-odds are in their favour. *Fortune* claims, 'They have been known to turn down big promotions or to quickly acquire clout and then give it all up for leisure.' It cautioned its readers – largely senior executives – that 'you might want to laugh derisively the first time one of your youngest subordinates tells you he intends to work a mere forty-hour week so he can go scuba-diving and learn a non-Indo-European tongue. But don't complain, then, when you can't seem to find another competent molecular biologist or quality-control specialist.'

For an article I was researching on the subject for *The Times* I sought out British 'yiffies' with similar sentiments. I was surprised to find so many willing to admit as much, particularly in industries such as advertising, in a period when company closures were almost constantly being announced and the so-called 'Thatcher's children', the thirty- and forty-something agency heads and creative directors, were tightening their belts and fearing for their Porsches.

Christopher Bain, a copywriter in his late twenties, and Andrew Plume, a twenty-five-year-old art director who worked with him, embodied the baby-buster mentality which could change the ethos of British industry over the coming decade. 'I know my priorities are totally different from those of my father, and even from my own of a few years ago,' said Bain, whose father, Nigel, was Head of Communications with the Institute of Personnel Management and an old-style workaholic who expressed himself amazed at how much time his son managed to take off to play golf.

Bain explained, 'I play for personal satisfaction and run a small golfing society for people like me in the business. Maybe we take six days off a year to play, as well as weekends and holidays. I think there's a clash of culture with people of my father's generation and those who were in advertising in the 1970s. Companies are closing and every day more redundancies are announced, so you have to be more intense about the time you spend at work – fool around less, have fewer long lunches – but you make more time for outside interests. And I don't have a single female friend who doesn't work full-time, so no one has the sort of support at home that the men who were sole breadwinners, like my father, used to expect.

'I spent the 1980s trying to further my own career, and then I began to ask, "Why am I doing this and who am I doing this for?"' Bain explained. 'Towards the end of the 1980s I began gearing everything towards retiring at the age of fifty, and started my first pension plan when I was twenty-five. Andrew [Plume] says he's going to retire at forty and almost everyone I know is looking forward to an earlier retirement than our parents' generation, and are trying to make some personal space in the meantime.'

Plume confirmed that he decided to retire at forty, 'while still at school. Not necessarily retire but take it easy – be open to new opportunities, like travelling. I thought I'd work hard now and then maybe take time off and see the world with my wife and children.' He wasn't married at the time, he added, but that was all part of the master plan.

It all sounds terribly holistic and humanistic (if a trifle calculating); the total antithesis of the work-aholic. But for every laid-back British 'yiffie' there's a 'whizzkid' who cut his or her teeth in the get-rich-quick 1980s and was weaned on the workaholic ethic.

In 1990 the National Curriculum Council recommended that pupils should be better schooled in 'enterprise and wealth', from the moment they started to 'play shops' in reception class – but many educators felt there already had been too much emphasis in this direction.

Bob Porter, assistant head of Highfields School in Matlock, Derbyshire, where young Christopher Peach was a pupil before the stock market crashed, leaving him and his parents with a reported £20,000 debt due to his extraordinary extra-curricular dealings, told me for an article I was doing on teenage entrepreneurs for *The Times* in August 1990, 'We are in danger of losing concern for the process in the quest for the product and we are producing a lot of little Thatcherites, not in the political sense, but who think that profit is the bottom line.'

Sixteen-year-old David Bolton abandoned – at least temporarily – his A levels in order to promote the computer program he had developed which looked set to revolutionize doctors' record-keeping and make him the country's youngest self-made millionaire.

Prior to his decision to leave school – which his headmaster, John Simpson, strenuously advised him against – Bolton had been driven there by his business agent in the Porsche he had earned but was too young to drive.

Simpson felt the boy's education was more precious than anything he could earn, but Professor John Radford, author of *Child Prodigies and Exceptional Early Achievers* (Harvester Wheatsheaf, 1990), expressed the opinion that David should seize the main chance and could 'always get his A-levels'.

Similarly, twelve-year-old James Harries of Cardiff gave up school to be tutored at times more convenient for running his antique and floristry businesses. James and his brothers Patrick and Adam are all young entrepreneurs who began thinking of playground schemes to make money and, at the time of writing, were planning to publish a magazine advising other businesses on how to survive the recession. James – who dresses in suits and bowties and is happier behind a desk than kicking a ball around – told me he loved his work and considered it much more fun than playing and more instructive than going to school.

Also in 1990 nineteen-year-old Spencer Trethewy – who called himself 'a property investment entrepreneur' – became an overnight celebrity by promising to save Aldershot Football Club with an investment of at least £100,000 of his own money, it was widely reported. Secretive about his business dealings, Trethewy – who claimed to have earned enough to rescue the team in just thirteen months of working – did tell me that his parents both owned their own companies and had probably passed the entrepreneurial spirit on to him, although he insisted they had not given him any actual financial help.

Trethewy had no plans for early retirement. 'I'm going to be around for thirty or forty years,' he boasted, 'and I've got very big plans!'

So had David Peller, who started his first business at the age of eight, running discos in a Sheffield hotel. At the time of writing he was masterminding a successful group of companies from the boys' call box at his public school, maintaining a working day that, he boasted, could last twenty hours. His turnover was estimated at around £500,000 a year from his two high-tech companies, supplying local authorities and private organizations with computer equipment, fax machines and mobile telephones, and a holding company.

Peller insisted that he was not working like this for the money. 'I am doing it for the experience, because I love it,' he said, with the glowing enthusiasm of the true workaholic. He felt the climate was more receptive than ever before to teenage tycoons, and that high-tech, low-overhead businesses such as his own were ideal for the first generation of computer children.

If the Thatcher era was a breeding-ground and nursery for them, many more will be making their marks in the 1990s.

Christine McNulty, chief executive of Applied Futures, a British firm whose business it is to predict social and corporate change, thinks it would be too simplistic to believe that either the 'Majorite' Christopher Bain and Andrew Plume or 'Thatcher's children' David Bolton and David Peller were in the vanguard of a single, dramatic mood shift which would sweep the nation towards the third millennium.

She believes that 'Margaret Thatcher and John Major represent the two types of inner-directed people who will *both* be at the leading edge of the future. She was one of those who find work so enjoyable they cannot separate it from leisure; he someone who finds fulfilment in activities outside his main job. We anticipate growth in both of these sorts of inner-directeds over the next decade.

'It is the workaholics who are not inner-directed but motivated by money, power or security – that is, the "outer-directed" or "sustenance-driven" work slaves – who are on the way out. These are the sort of people who keep their heads down and work frantically to earn their Porsche or their first million or to prove themselves a success in the eyes of their peers. They are not people of vision and personal commitment like Mrs Thatcher, although they have been called Thatcher's children. And leadership, which we will require more of than management in the 1990s, demands the sort of vision and charisma that only an inner-directed worker can provide.' Of the two types of inner-directed workers who will be at the leading edge of the future, McNulty says, 'One will never want to retire and the other will want to retire early because they have so many interests to pursue.'

Society will have to learn to make provision for them both, so that no one is made to stay on unwillingly at work and no one forced into premature retirement, which can be – it is fairly generally acknowledged – as great a killer as overwork. Then we would come closer to the philosophy of Kahlil Gibran, author of *The Prophet*, that 'Work is love made visible, and if you cannot work with love but only with distaste, it is better that you should leave your work

and sit at the gate of the temple and take alms of those who work with joy.'

But McNulty notes that at the moment approximately 63 per cent – a significant proportion – of the nation is still outer-directed or sustenance-driven, and would welcome the signals that slowing down and 'mellowing out', as the Americans call it, is more permissible than it was in the Thatcher era.

To that degree Mr Major – like his boating, fishing counterpart across the Atlantic, George Bush – was heralded as a welcome role model for the executive of the 1990s; not arrogant enough to consider himself indispensable but with too sound a sense of self-worth to allow himself to be used as if he were expendable, and too many irons in the fire to become burnt-out.

A number of surveys attempted to predict the working mood of the 1990s at the dawn of the decade, and gave out confusing and contradictory messages. A report published in mid-1989 by the executive search consultants Saxton Bampfylde International profiled the ideal 'Euro-executive', who would be required, the headhunters insisted, to lead Britain to success in the European Community in 1992. Existing ones would be 'married to a long-suffering Euro-wife who has uncomplainingly raised his multi-lingual children without adding to his stress level by nagging about his incessant travelling,' I reported in *The Times*.

Those earmarked for future development into the leaders of the 1990s were serious Euro-workaholics such as Eleanor Buss, at the time a twenty-six-year-old investment analyst with a London-based 'Euro-bank', who maintained, 'I'm trying not to think about marriage and children because I see myself perpetually missing my daughter's birthday and my son's sports day.' Or Thomas Scott-Morey, a thirty-one-year-old banker who always carried an international flight guide, lived on the Heathrow side of London for easy egress and kept a set of major European currencies in his wallet because 'nothing speaks louder than cash'. He spoke French, Italian and Cantonese but always talked finance in English, he said, 'because that's the one area in which you can't afford to be misunderstood'.

The 'Spoilt Brats' report produced by the advertising agency Gold Greenlees Trott at the turn of the decade predicted that the next generation, weaned on *Wall Street* and a 'loadsamoney' ethos, would be mainly composed of money-grubbing mini-moguls caring only about getting rich quick.

This was disconcertingly at odds with other more ideological projections for the supposedly 'caring, sharing' 1990s. One survey, for example, of sixth formers in the South-east, indicated that the pupils of the 1980s, who would be workers of the 1990s, would place happiness and health way ahead of wealth on their list of priorities. Careers in fashions and music came top of the pops, not banking and finance.

Other surveys heralded the rise of the self-employed entrepreneur – a role increasing numbers of women were finding attractive as they struggled to juggle family commitments in a workaholic whirl. One by the accountancy firm Kidsons Impney in 1990 revealed that although two-thirds of new entre-preneurs were married, 68 per cent said they would put business before family and fewer than 30 per cent said they achieved a 'well-balanced mix'. While money was the motivation for almost 40 per cent, 29 per cent of those questioned said it was the desire for a sense of control, being their own boss, that spurred them on, and 28 per cent said they were motivated by the challenge of running a business. Yet two-thirds also said they intended to retire before the age of fifty.

When the transatlantic 'priority management' consultant Dan Stamp, president of Priority Manage-ment Systems Inc, surveyed 1,300 executives in eight countries, he discovered that they put 'more time with family', 'good health', 'more time for myself' and 'more knowledge' in many cases above 'more money'. Only 35 per cent of those questioned said salary would be *more* important to them in the year 2000. And a survey of executives in leading British companies by Professor Cary Cooper published in 1991 revealed that nearly 50 per cent of senior executives felt their jobs were interfering with their social and family lives – whereas only 22 per cent had responded that way in a similar survey he conducted in 1984.

But as I said earlier, surveys can prove just about

anything. Reality probably lies somewhere between the most idealistic and most pessimistic visions of the 1990s, with elements of truth from each.

The teenage tycoon David Peller voiced one very perceptive prediction of his own. 'One of the problems will be that so many young people – like me – are moving into *secondary* industries, not production industries, which will do the balance of trade no good. It may sound terrible, but if you try to turn everyone into a bourgeois snob who runs his own business, who is going to *work*?'

4

High Tech, High Stress, High Status?

*'Work as if you were to live a hundred years; pray as
if you were to die tomorrow.'*

Benjamin Franklin

'Burn out' was a phrase that became all to common in
the 1980s. It was a time when high tech led to high
stress, which was perceived as high status and left
many high-flyers feeling highly drained.

The rise of the cellular phone and fax machine
meant that it was increasingly difficult to switch off
from work. The electronic Psion personal organizer
supplemented, if it didn't quite supplant, the bulging
Filofax and the advent of tele-working, made possible
through personal computers linked into office main-
frames, meant that an Englishman's (or woman's)
home was no longer a fortress of solitude and opened
up new horizons for 'homeworkers'.

Even as I write a form has come through my door
from Blue Arrow Personnel Services, asking whether
I would like to work for 'top pay' in the comfort of my
own home. I must let them know whether I can
operate a VDU or word-processor, specifying 'model
and package' and whether I have the space at home to

install one.

As a freelance journalist I work from home, and it sometimes surprises people that I can have a cosmopolitan career based in an obscure little village in the Midlands. Admittedly there are excellent rail and road networks near where I live, but I transmit much of my work through computer modems and receive vital material by fax.

The fax machine is, 'for the moment' (as I've been saying for the past two years), by the bed, since there's not another available phone point in my office, with several lines in there already. *I* think it doubles nicely as a bedside telephone – and there's even a spot on it to rest my specs – but my husband finds it, even silent and unplugged, intrusive. He was not amused one night to arrive home unexpectedly around midnight to discover me sitting up excitedly in bed receiving some lengthy scrolls of information I'd just requested from Utah.

I had to hastily explain that I'd only taken such a liberty since he'd been away – and from his expression I'm not sure he wouldn't rather have been surprised by a secret lover. We were both reminded of the scene in *Campaign*, the British television series that tried to sum up life in an advertising agency in the 1980s, in which the irate husband rips out the answering machine he views as the umbilical cord that links his wife with her office. The scene struck a responsive chord with us.

Now that cordless phones and lap-top computers are commonplace, it is possible for me to conduct my business from the garden on a summer's day or curled up on the sofa in winter. I am no longer confined to my desk. As a workaholic, I feel this makes working so

much more convenient – so much more *fun*. There's
hardly any need to stop! But other family members
aren't quite so sure, and – being, I hope, a rational
workaholic – I can understand their reservations.

Just as the video telephone, if it ever comes into
common use, will be a brilliant breakthrough with the
potential to become an irksome invasion of privacy, so
the advent of each piece of personal, portable office
equipment brings new problems and pressures.

Now that new technology makes working quicker
and easier and it is possible to receive and process
information almost instantly from around the world,
the old excuses, such as 'It's in the post', no longer
wash. Great expectations create greater pressures,
and there are very few times now that anyone can say
it's impossible to get any work done – 'It'll have to wait
until Monday morning.' As one leading New York
lawyer told *Fortune* magazine last year, 'We used to
type off drafts of contracts on seven-page carbons, and
by 9.30 at night you had to give them to the typing
pool. Then you went home . . . [now] we can print out
a contract, fax it to London, and wait around until 3
am when they've finished reviewing it and we can
start working on it again.'

The *Wall Street*-style yuppies of the 1980s burnt out,
like the young hero of the film, from the impossible
strain of attempting to keep up with money markets
around the world – early-morning calls to Tokyo, late-
night messages from LA, and London and New York
to cope with in between. Electronic paging systems
meant that it was impossible to be 'incommunicado',
and insistent bleeps marred 'off-duty' moments for
salesmen as well as surgeons. The ultimate absurdity
came early in 1991, when a tycoon accused of stealing

millions of pounds from his own company was let out
on what the papers called a 'yuppie bail' – the
stipulation that he would always carry a mobile
telephone so that the police could check up on him. In
an era which saw so many tycoons on trial and in jail, it
was probably not as silly as it initially sounded.

According to British Telecom the Gulf War saw a
surge in 'videoconferencing'. Whereas this service –
which costs a minimum of £100 from a BT centre and a
minimum of £20,000 for those wishing to rent
equipment for their offices – was doubling its
turnover annually, after 15 January 1991 it shot up 'an
additional 60 per cent on top of that,' a BT spokesman
told me, 'because people were afraid of travelling.'
With international terrorism now a constant threat, it
may continue to do well, and there is a scheme afoot to
make facilities more readily available through local
chambers of commerce 'not as a travel substitute but
to generate business for small companies who
couldn't afford that scale of travel in the first place,'
says the international solicitor John Brebner of
Brebner & Co. who is promoting the project.

In America – where some young children go around
with electronic pagers clipped to their baseball caps
and belts – executive cars have long been fitted with
portable fax machines and computers as well as
telephones, and it is not unusual to see desks
instead of bars being used by the passengers in those
obscenely opulent 'stretch' limousines. *The Times*
reported in May 1990 that Steven Syfers, a real-estate
agent in California, had bought one equipped with
two computers in addition to all the usual mod cons,
and that an entire company called Commuter Products
Ltd had sprung up to help workaholic commuters

make the most of their time. (More frivolous products included an electronic message board which would flash rude notes across the bumper and a massaging car seat.) 'The bottom line is the need of businesspeople to use their time and use it productively and to be in touch while on the road,' Michael Meresman, editor of an American magazine responding to this need, called *Mobile Office*, told *The Times*.

'Car-cooning', as it was called, was the mobile equivalent of cocooning, a word developed by the American 'futurist' Faith Popcorn of Brain Reserve, who has demonstrated a deft way with words ever since changing her name from Plotkin. She predicted that people would be staying at home more in the 1990s, and working from home more in the 1990s precisely because the technology would exist to facilitate such cocooning, with electronic umbilical cords to almost every facility in the outside world. With technology for complete home office and leisure systems becoming more sophisticated every day (pioneers at the Media Lab of the Massachusetts Institute of Technology have just produced laser-generated three-dimensional images that appear to float in the air – created purely from computer data – bringing us a step closer to the futuristic world of Ray Bradbury's *Illustrated Man*), the concept of cocooning could hold increasing attraction. But as technology intrudes into new areas, it will create new stresses – including the one Dr David Lewis calls 'technophobia', from which, apparently, many of us suffer. (Professor Cary Cooper's recent study of the stress levels of top civil servants, for example, showed that they found queuing at the photocopier more stressful than tackling more sophisticated procedures.)

In the era of electric treadmills and electronic
rowing simulators, there wasn't even the get-out that
the weather was too bad to go jogging in the wee
hours before or after work – and true workaholics
who don't like to stop working while working-out
keep television screens showing stock-market figures
positioned above their exercise bicycles – an extra
endurance test for the ticker.

International jewellery magnate Gerald Ratner, a
work enthusiast who also places a high priority on
fitness, keeps several screens always switched on in
the well-equipped gymnasium he has installed in the
basement of his lavish central London headquarters;
and 'executive' health clubs use them as a selling-point
to lure time-urgent, workaholic members. Five years

ago British business travellers were amazed when American hotels boasted such facilities, and didn't hesitate to put business calls through to the gym at ungodly hours so that deals could be clinched as waists were cinched on to exercise machines. Now such service is expected in Britain too.

The development of supersonic travel made it possible for moguls to machinate and masticate on both sides of the Atlantic in a single day, 'red-eye' flights became *de rigueur* for middle managers (who were not allowed the luxury of jetlag – a fear one cunning British Airways commercial played on) and the pace of business life was heightened to an unprecedented level. Just as world leaders were expected to be able to negotiate instantly upon arrival at a summit – no matter how far they had flown or how long experts felt it should technically take the human body to adjust – so business people began to feel they had to act like Superman when they began flying almost as frequently as the fictional Man of Steel.

In 1990 an 'international consultant' called Fred Finn had 'registered an incredible 9,975,000 miles on his body clock,' the *Daily Mail* reported, and was gearing himself up to become 'ten-million-mile man'. Finn, forty-nine at the time, attributed the break-up of his first marriage to the strain his constant travelling put on his wife, and admitted, 'I suppose I have wasted more of my life than I can really afford encased in an aluminium tube.' But he met his second wife when he was given a party to mark his 600th Concorde flight in Simpsons of Piccadilly, where she was the ground-floor manageress – and they married at an open-air altar on a beach in Jamaica.

'It's probably true that I spent more time in planes than I did with my ex-wife,' Finn reflected. 'But with Rosita I take her with me, even if it's only for a night in New York.' Other workaholic commuters who, like Finn, merit their own seat in the 'Concorde Club' include Lord Weidenfeld and David Frost.

But a book published in the same year, *The Curse of Icarus* (Routledge, 1990), by Farrol Kahn, another man with his fingers in many professional pies, warned that frequent flying could exacerbate almost every ailment, from asthma to toothache, and exposes us to too much radiation. When I asked the author about businesspeople and world leaders who had to fly frequently as part of their jobs, he responded, 'No one can be in a fit state to do business after a long flight. As a general rule, for every time zone we cross it takes one day to recover. Airline pilots go off-duty on arrival, whereas diplomats, athletes and executives have to demonstrate efficiency at their destination.'

Professor Malcolm Harrington, director of the Institute of Occupational Health at the University of Birmingham, told me when I spoke to him for an article on the health of summit leaders for *The Times* in 1988, that as far as he was concerned the major occupational hazard facing the leaders was the travelling they do. 'Do we really want the fate of the world in the hands of someone with jet-lag?' he demanded, and warned against the dangers of someone going straight into an important meeting, 'when they're not cerebrating terribly well and decision-making certainly isn't at its best'.

Professor Cooper, co-author of *Pilots Under Stress* (Routledge, 1986), a study of the physical and mental health of 500 commercial airline pilots, says he doubts that anyone can function effectively at the end of a long flight. Yet world leaders – and businesspeople like Mr Finn – continue to have to do so, in a workaholic whirl encapsulated by the American Express 'I've got to get *back* to Bahrain *tonight!*' commercial of the 1980s.

Will there be a backlash in the 1990s against all this high tech, leading to high stress, which is perceived as high status? Even the most workaholic (and tech-noholic) experts are predicting that there *must* be, despite an apparent demographic need for a dwindling pool of workers to work increasingly hard. (The sharp decline in birthrate during the 1970s means that there should be a shortfall during this decade of over a million young workers in their late teens and early twenties compared with the 1980s.)

Health scares about flying were compounded by those linked to other sophisticated electrical and electronic devices creating electromagnetic fields. There were whispers that working too intensely with computers might encourage the development of brain cancer – which, the *American Journal of Industrial Medicine* reported in 1990, was mysteriously on the increase. Chemicals used in photocopiers and laser printers and other high-tech office equipment were said to contribute to so-called 'sick building' syndrome, which flourished in both Britain and America in the 1980s – further encouragement to 'tele-commuting'. And a host of other high-tech ailments were discovered, from VDU-operator's eye to word-processor's wrist. The latest scare concerns mobile telephones: one GP made headlines for alleging that they could cause anything from brain tumours and leukaemia to personality changes because they send radio waves through the brain. The doctor claimed his practice, which dealt primarily with over-worked executives, was overrun by people whose problems could be attributed to over-use of mobile phones. Although British Telecom emphatically denied that there could be any health risk associated with using mobile phones – except 'if you are using one while walking down the street and bump into a lamp-post,' as one witty spokesperson put it – the Solihull doctor's findings echo an earlier call from Scandinavia for health warnings to be put on mobile phones. In any case, as we entered the 90s all the signs were that even for those who had most enthusiastically embraced the new technology, the honeymoon period was over and a holiday was needed.

In the series of articles in *The Times* called 'Home from Home', to which I contributed regularly during 1990, about the rural retreats of those well-off enough to enjoy such a luxury, the most distinctive distinguishing feature between workaday and week-end homes seemed to be the home-from-home's relative inaccessibility by telephone and fax machine.

Moyses Stevens Group chairman Jennifer d'Abo would tolerate a fax machine in her hideaway on a stately estate, but wouldn't allow business contacts to know her phone number there. 'The fax doesn't intrude like the telephone does,' she explained. 'I can decide when to look at the faxes.' High priestess of the Hip and Thigh Diet, Rosemary Conley, had bought a hideaway home-from-home just half an hour's drive from her main residence, simply because she felt it was no longer possible to relax in a house that was so hooked into her business, with phone and fax lines constantly buzzing. 'Nobody is going to have the telephone number here,' she vowed – before entrusting it to me. 'But we have had to keep a fax and computer here just to keep in touch. We have to be practical,' she added.

The unapologetically workaholic headhunter Jo Cutmore, who runs her own highly successful business, confided that she was having to have a *second* retreat built in France, primarily to escape the demands of phone and fax which follow her family to their Norfolk cottage at weekends. And she had originally chosen *that* cottage 'because it was out of cell-phone range – now *that's* remote!'

Professor Charles Handy, visiting professor at the London Business School, vice-president of the Royal Society of Arts and one of Britain's great management gurus, told me how he and his wife, Elizabeth, relished the slower rhythm of their farm labourer's cottage in East Anglia, which was a complete change from their sophisticated London home. 'When people come to stay with us here it's very relaxed,' Mrs Handy said, 'whereas in London one tends to see work friends.' But the work friends, she added anxiously, were beginning to beat a path to their country door with increasing frequency – aided and abetted by improved railway services and fax and telephone lines. 'We have to stay linked up,' she said ruefully, 'because of Charles's work. Wherever we were we'd have to have that. But now we're thinking we may have to buy a *third* house just to *really* get away from it all!'

Dr John Nicholson, the business psychologist who advised British Telecom on its advertisement campaign designed to convince workaholics that the phone could take at least some of their strain, says, 'Six or seven years ago I used to beg people at the top of

companies to give away car phones, telling them that
the gesture would repay itself many times over. Now
people two levels down are begging me *not* to
recommend they be given car phones because the
pressure it creates is too great and being in their car
was one of the few times they could escape.'

But six years ago cell phones had not saturated the
strata of mediocre middle management as they have
today. Now that every salesman and building-site
supervisor struts about with one, and *second*-class
railway carriages are filled with pompous poseurs
phoning their offices to convey such urgent messages
as, 'I'm on my way . . . We'll be arriving at Euston in
ten minutes . . . I'll phone you again when I'm in the
taxi . . .' the technology has lost considerable cachet.
Taxation could prove its death knell.

Whereas once it was such a status symbol to receive
a phone call in a restaurant that aspiring starlets and
their agents would conspire to have themselves
ostentatiously paged in all the best places, a growing
number of top restaurants in Britain and America are
banning their customers from using cellular phones at
the table because they believe it lowers the tone.

It caused a stir when portable phones were considered too crude, too crassly, 'working' class, to be
allowed into the swish steward's enclosure at the
Henley Regatta in 1990 – one of the traditional
bastions of the 'leisured' classes which the British
'season' is meant to attract, but which has, in recent
years, become open season for 'corporate hospitality'.
('Corporate hospitality', which peaked, plateaued and
plummeted during the 1980s, can be a skiving 'jolly'
for funloving freeloaders – or a workaholic way of
mixing business with pleasure. For some participants

it is the former, but for many it is, quite genuinely, the latter – although the Inland Revenue does not regard it in that light, just as the plan to tax mobile phones as a perk, because it was assumed people would make personal calls on them, failed to take into account the fact that such devices in the hand of a workaholic erode any remnant of 'personal' life.)

London taxicabs, which optimistically installed expensive passenger phones in the late 1980s, have nearly all had them removed because – the cabbies complain – they were seldom used, since all their customers either had their own or found the concept repellent.

Hard on the heels of a Mintel survey of 'personal telecommunications' which predicted that the already £2 billion UK market for 'mobile telecommunications services' would almost double to £3.9 billion by 1993, the *Daily Telegraph* reported in February 1991: 'Recession pulls the plug on mobile phones', with 'phones . . . surrendered in rising numbers'. The fax market, Mintel reported, had also slowed, with 'sales originally predicted to run at about 1,000 a day during 1989' turning out 'to be closer to 650', and the 'much predicted home market' failing to materialize – despite continually lowering prices.

So, as Bob Tyrrell of the Henley Centre of Forecasting once predicted, workaholics who carry their offices on their backs may shortly seem absurd anachronisms, ridiculous figures of fun (as in the Russ Abbott comedy sketch about the man so laden down with portable phones that he doesn't know which one is ringing).

Tyrrell told me when I asked him and other 'futurists' to make their predictions for the 1990s towards the end of 1989, 'It will be smart to seem *unbusy* in the 1990s. In the 1980s all the accoutrements of business and facilitators of busy lives have had high status: Filofaxes, faxes, portable telephones, etc. This was an exception to the long-term norm, which is for the *leisured* classes to be smart.' This prediction obviously delighted many of the still leisured readers of *Harpers & Queen*, the top people's magazine, for which I wrote up the predictions!

Tyrrell further prophesied that this attitude shift would hit the convenience-food industry and many other goods and services which had been popular in the 1980s because they were considered 'time saving'. 'At the moment we're doing a lot of "time saving" and then wasting it,' Tyrrell pointed out. 'The "smart" person will save time without blind purpose.'

Faith Popcorn confirmed Tyrrell's hunches – but for slightly different reasons. 'By the year 2000 the "Me Decade" will be replaced by a concern for the environment and a return to old-fashioned values, which will be reflected in the appliances and equipment we buy,' she told me.

But in this transitional phase before we return, if we do, to the blank piece of paper and pencil and home-baked apple pie, an equally formidable high-tech industry has grown up to cope with the high stress generated partly by all the high tech. In both Britain and America companies with names such as Synchro Energize Salon and The Universe of You promise stress reduction and enduring serenity if you slip on their strange goggles, watch flashing lights and listen to special tunes. For those who don't want to relax the same machines are said to help boost memory, job and sports performance and, as *Time* magazine reported in 1990, there is even a home model called InnerQuest.

As already mentioned in Chapter 2, Professor Cary Cooper was amazed by the correspondence he received from angry individuals whose occupations had rated low on the list of his occupational stress tables. The association of stress with status surprised Cooper, particularly since, as he never fails to emphasize, 'A sense of *control* is crucial in minimizing occupational stress, and it is often those in low-status jobs, with little control over their working lives, who are the most stressed, even though stress is *perceived* as an executive disease.'

He has since explored the connection further, along with the hundreds of high-tech stress-relief devices which have replaced that earlier and more innocent status symbol, the executive toy (but which are more likely to be bought by those with frustrated aspirations to executivity). Companies with names such as Stresswise, Stress X and Pocket Freud have identified a market gap just screaming out to be filled – many of them using 1980s technology to cure some of the ills of 1980s technology.

A swift survey of department stores during the pre-Christmas 1990 period revealed scores of so-called stress-relief devices, meant to be picked up as stocking-fillers by those supposed to be scrabbling for Psion organizers, portable photocopiers and solar-powered calculators, and for their offspring, toddlers' 'talking computers' and cot-side cell phones.

There were electronic screaming balls, which emitted a hollow howl like a soul in torment and were marketed as 'a prescription for stress', and 'Wham-It' inflatable punching bags, which came self-importantly packaged as 'an anti-stress device'. There were 'frustration bricks', which could be hurled satisfyingly across a room without causing any harm, 'stress relief baseballs' – ditto, and obviously an American import, like so many of these products, including 'Tearapart' bosses, to be dismembered with the satisfying sound of ripping Velcro 'when you're stressed-out to the max'.

There were numerous things to squeeze and crush ('Smooshables' came in the shape of bosses, mothers-in-law and other hate figures), and for truly sadistic stress-sufferers the 'Whacko' cockroach, that was designed to cringe quietly on your desk until it was hammered on the head in a moment of workday rage, when it would squeak and run about. ('Poor Mr X,' a little man who worked on a similar principle, pathetically cried, 'Oh, oh, forgive me, please,' when he was beaten – no doubt to give the low-status worker delusions of power and control over an inferior being!)

'The Final Word', a pocket calculator-like device, promised to say the sort of things to your boss you're supposed to have wished you had the courage to say, while the 'Freud Talking Pillow' suggested: 'Press me to relieve your worry so I can worry and fuss out loud.'

'Bio-feedback' devices of various sorts were being promoted by mail order, such as Biodots, adhesive dots which stick to the fingers and supposedly show you how relaxed you are by the amount of circulation in your extremities. If they don't give off a warm glow, you are supposed to do some swift relaxation exercises until they do.

And then there was 'Stress Man', billed as an 'instant' relaxation device which was said to send 'mild electronic impulses to an exact treatment point on the upper ear for those too stressed to stop and relax'.

Even previously innocent children's toys such as skipping ropes and basketball sets took on a sinister double entendre when repackaged as stress-prevention aids. There was the 'stress-relief basketball' game Harrods was promoting (remember how the angst-ridden Michael and Elliot of *Thirtysomething* used to take their business and personal frustrations out on their office set?), or the 'Executive Rap-n-rope', called 'the ultimate stress-escape technique'.

The anti-stress gadgets seemed to fall roughly into three categories: those which provided an outlet for anger and frustration; those that encouraged a displacement activity involving some sort of exercise or skill; and those which would give a warning signal, which is meant to trigger a change in behaviour.

For an article I wrote on the subject for *The Times* I asked three of Britain's leading stress experts, Professor Cooper, Dr Malcolm Carruthers and Dr David Lewis, what they thought of such supposed stress-relief devices and whether they only added to the stress of our high-tech, high-pressure existence.

Dr Carruthers, the stress specialist who runs a Positive Health Centre in London's Harley Street and teaches autogenic training, was least perturbed by the profusion of gadgets purporting to be able to do so much for so many for so little. He had been involved, he said, with the development of a wristwatch, to be launched in 1991, which would be able to measure pulse and blood pressure, and envisaged the day when 'we can have this facility built into the steering wheel of a car, so that an audible alarm goes off as a warning to pull over and calm down when your pulse or blood pressure gets dangerously high'.

He believes that the advantages of such a scheme would outweigh its obvious disadvantages, just as he feels that the benefits of joky stress-relief devices, however gimmicky, should not be laughed off. 'Anything that helps let off steam is a good idea,' he told me. 'When I teach autogenic training, I teach people how to have a proper temper tantrum and how to cry – and the only bad thing is that some of these devices are making the noises that the stressed person should be making himself in order to let off steam. Japanese companies have gymnasia with punching bags with the faces of the managing director on them and employees can go there during their lunch hour, punch and grunt and take out their aggression and emerge smiling.' He had apparently suggested such a technique would come in useful in the House of Commons gymnasium!

The Japanese apparently also have the word *karoshi* in their language, meaning 'death by overwork', and the transatlantic 'priority management' proponent, Dan Stamp, believes the Western world should appropriate it, and use 'karoshed' to describe anyone who dies from stress or associated health problems due to overwork. Stamp, whose report on *The 21st Century Workplace* was published in 1990, found in his survey of 1,300 business people in eight countries that while 94 per cent had a computer in their office, 36 per cent lacked the skill to operate it – which must in itself have caused some stress – and that 66 per cent said their workplace was more stressful than it had been ten years ago, partly due to new technology.

Dr Lewis, a psychologist who founded the charity Stress Watch and is an industry consultant on stress, picked up the same Japanese analogy – but with more scepticism. 'Some of these stress toys seem to me rather sadistic things that are a Westernized version of the Japanese punching bags,' he observed.'Although I agree that it's probably better to kick plastic than a person, I believe that anger *out* is as bad as anger *in* and that toys which encourage hostility are not healthy.'

Dr Lewis, like Dr Carruthers, was more intrigued by the bio-feedback devices, 'which tell people something about their state of tension and may encourage them to do something about it. But often these generally available ones, such as Biodots and Stress Cards that you can place your thumb on, are not really all that accurate and they can worry people unnecessarily,' he cautioned. For his own workshops in 'creative stress' he favours little trains which can be moved about by the alpha-waves Type A executives are trained to relax enough in order to produce.

Professor Cooper, author of numerous books on stress and occupational health, believes we should be asking not what these anti-stress devices can do for us but what can be done about a society which has spawned them. 'The growth industry in these silly items is telling us something serious about the times we live in,' he says. 'It tells you this must be a significant issue. And you will notice that a lot of these toys are now being UK-initiated, whereas originally they were all from the United States. This reflects the way Britain has moved, over the past decade, into a much more competitive, enterprise culture.'

The move has also been, he noted, from so called 'executive toys', which were simply aesthetically pleasing status symbols, into those supposedly designed to alleviate what is now generally considered the highest status symbol – stress.

'There's a funny side to these "executive" toys, but there's a serious hidden message if you're given one,' Professor Cooper warned. 'It's, "Do you realize that this is the way I perceive you and others perceive you?" So take note. If someone gives you a punchbag, they are showing you that they perceive you to be aggressive – and that's the first-stage symptom of stress. If someone gives you a Biodot, it could show that they are genuinely worried about your health.' So the gimmick could become a catalyst for change even if it, *per se*, is not seriously effective against stress.

But well-meaning buyers should also beware, Professor Cooper cautioned. 'The thing about these toys is that too many of them are achievement-oriented – even if it's only trying to get a spot to turn green. They could cause more stress in the competitive Type A personalities they are meant to calm.'

So the time-urgent, workaholic whirl of the 1980s spawned a high-tech, highly stressed generation misguided enough to mistake stress for status – and to crave them both. Why some people thrive on such stress, while others die from it, can provide the crucial clues which help to distinguish the dynamo from the drone.

5

Healthy Enthusiasm Or Sick Obsession?

'In order that people may be happy in their work these
three things are needed: they must be fit for it, they
must not do too much of it, and they must have a sense
of success in it.'

John Ruskin

Workaholism, we are warned, can be hazardous to the health. But if you're going to kill yourself through any sort of over-indulgence, it's probably the most productive way to go. It's arguably better than hitting the bottle or gorging on junk food or popping a pill for every ill, and surely no more foolish than overdoing exercise or putting oneself at risk through dangerous sports or pastimes. (Although the more dangerous manifestations of workaholism, some experts suggest, can lead to other areas of addiction in order to support or provide a counterpoint to the workaholic's intense involvement with work.)

The coronary-care units are supposed to be crammed with burnt-out workaholics who have blown a fuse – competitive Type A types who have to be taught how to slow down. The most hopeless cases are said even to do their recommended relaxation exercises in a competitive, achievement-oriented way. And an increasing number of women are becoming victims of heart disease, from which pre-menopausal females were largely considered to be protected; this is partly due, experts have suggested, to their increased burden of executive responsibility. Acquiring men's diseases along with their jobs, is how this syndrome has been reported – often with a sense of smug satisfaction.

Dr Jan de Winter of the Cancer Prevention Foundation in Brighton believes that the higher levels of sex hormones apparently found in high-achieving women can trigger cancers of the breast and womb. The presence of such hormones, however, according to Professor Cary Cooper's findings, does little for their sex lives, which, he has gone on record as stating, are 'virtually non-existent' – for reasons which will be explored more fully later.

Professor Cooper observes, 'Women used to be more prone to neuroses when they were frustrated by being at home. Now that they are going out to work, and raising a family, their mental health problems are decreasing but they are starting to get "male" diseases like heart disease. Evidence from the United States shows that heart disease rates among working women with children are sharply on the increase.'

Yet at the same time Cooper's research seemed to indicate that ambitious career women are *less* likely to get breast cancer than their stay-at-home sisters. Cooper questioned over 2,000 women aged between twenty and seventy who went for breast screening, and he showed that the typical Type-A committed careerwoman had less risk of the disease than her patient, uncompetitive Type-B counterpart, who was more likely to bottle things up. However, he found that the stress of a loss – such as redundancy – could make these women more prone to the disease. 'We are not saying cancer is caused by this,' he told the *Psychological Medicine Journal* in 1990, 'but that the immune system may fail when there is a stressful or loss-related event, especially if the personality cannot seek out support.'

He defined Type-A women as time-urgent, competitive, anticipating what other people are trying to say (and trying to complete sentences for them), likely to attempt to do too many things at once, faster eaters and walkers, ambitious and anxious to achieve recognition, and with few interests outside work. Type Bs were more casual about time-keeping, not so competitive, good listeners, able to wait patiently and take one thing at a time, slow, deliberate talkers, easygoing, unambitious and with many interests besides work. They *seemed* to be under much less stress. But stress is not always what it seems.

On several occasions when Dr Malcolm Carruthers hooked up a housewife and mother and her supposedly high-powered businessman husband to electronic equipment designed to measure stress levels, the stay-at-home housewife and mother had demonstrably higher levels of stress (something other housewives and mothers could have told him).

When I did a feature for *The Times* on 'the school runs' – following several mothers through days which needed to be planned with the precision of military campaigns as they dropped off and picked up several offspring at different educational establishments and fitted in play sessions and music and dancing lessons in between – it was easy to see why.

No one would deny that overwork can lead to a host of debilitating physical and psychological illnesses – if it is not done with that exhilarating sense of enthusiasm that the *healthy* and well-adjusted work-aholic experiences. Stress-related illnesses – as great a plague of the 1980s as Aids – usually occur when the exhilaration is gone. They manifest themselves in many ways.

As I wrote in the *Sunday Express Magazine* in 1990, 'Some people get skin rashes, others suffer palpitations, shortness of breath and temper, hair loss, sleeplessness – or chronic sleepiness. In extreme cases stress is thought to suppress the immune system in much the same way as the Aids virus does, leaving its victims more vulnerable to coughs, colds and even cancer. It raises the cholesterol level and lowers the libido. It is thought to be implicated in multiple sclerosis, diabetes and heart disease, as well as in premature ageing, obesity, alcoholism and accidents. As Dr Carruthers, author of *The Western Way of Death*, says, "I believe it is the number-one killer in the Western world and the most important contributory factor to heart and circulatory disease. It's what's eating you that matters much more than what you eat!"'

ME – Myalgic Encephalomyelitis – a mysterious ailment which surfaced during the 1980s, was nicknamed Yuppie flu because its 'chronic fatigue syndrome' seemed to strike precisely that type of hard-working high-achiever – the sort who would never take a holiday until their body packed up for them. If Aids was regarded by some finger-pointing moralists as a punishment for the promiscuity of previous decades, ME – which claimed such high-profile victims as the yachtswoman turned novelist

Clare Francis – was seen as the perfect form of retribution for the workaholic 1980s: Nature's way of telling workaholics to slow down.

The *Sunday Express*'s medical editor, Neville Hodgkinson, reported in a 'health focus' on the disease early in 1991, 'There is now overwhelming evidence that in most cases, so-called ME is a condition of chronic physical strain brought about by excessive mental and emotional burdens. Sufferers are victims of a vicious circle in which the mental strain puts their bodies into a state of red alert, as though they were about to be run over by a bus.' They might have been driven to this state, he suggested, by 'unacknowledged limitations at work or in relationships'.

But it is equally important to remember that idleness can be a killer too – and that enforced idleness, in the form of unemployment or redundancy, has been found to be as great a cause of stress as the most high-powered job. The number of working days lost because malingerers whose hearts – healthy or not – aren't in their jobs might tip the balance in favour of the committed worker.

Professor Cooper's research into the health effects of retirement and redundancy showed that whereas retired people had no particular health problems (and that 40 per cent of them chose to continue in some sort of occupation after their official retirement) redundancy or enforced retirement could 'cause all sorts of problems', from depression to heart attacks. And in a paper in the *British Journal of Industrial Medicine* in 1989 Professor Richard Schilling suggested that we should view 'work itself as a protector and promoter of health. For some people work offers opportunities for creative and stimulating activity. For the many who have dull, uninspiring jobs, it provides a base for establishing social contacts and companionship. Conversely, there is strong evidence that unemployment is damaging to the health.'

'Pick of the Week' presenter Margaret Howard, summarily axed after 17 years with the programme, told Valerie Grove of the *Sunday Times*: 'I was rather stunned and feeling ill. It makes you ill, you know, being fired. No wonder men go into a terrible decline when they lose their jobs. Your identity goes. It's not just the money. It's the whole persona, swept away.'

Professor Schilling, eighty at the time of writing and Emeritus Professor of Occupational Health at London University, told me he attributed his active long life to 'the fact that I'm still under slight pressure, using my mind. That's an important factor in longevity.' In his paper he makes the point that 'Women's superior longevity over men begins at retiring age and gradually increases. Nearly 88 per cent of the over-100 age group in England and Wales are women. The causes underlying this sex difference are complex. Cyril Clarke, an eminent physician and geneticist, suggests one reason why women live longer. There is no retirement for them whereas many men, after gainful employment ceases, become less active both physically and mentally.'

Dr Richard Smith, author of *Unemployment and Health* (Oxford University Press, 1987) and executive editor of the *British Medical Journal*, notes that, 'Suicide is two to two and a half times commoner among the unemployed – as are many types of accidents and cancers, particularly lung cancer.' He also told me that, 'Most people's mental health deteriorates after losing their jobs, and the 10 per cent who don't deteriorate usually have some particularly important reason for living apart from their employment: maybe they are very religious, or politically committed.' There is also evidence that the unemployed are generally less physically healthy, and that they smoke and drink more than their employed equivalents – regardless of social class.

There are as many stress-related diseases linked to being out of work as to having too much work – and not only because of financial difficulties. One Bristol doctor told me, 'I once knew two friends who were employed on full salaries but had no work coming in for a while. They were both very positive people usually and it was quite interesting seeing what happened to them without work: they both became very negative.' And a London commuter-belt GP told me, 'The whole family breaks up when businesses are put under pressure and jobs are lost. They present with chest pains and migraines – somatic symptoms which are really caused by stress. Their spouses and children come in more frequently too. It's a different kind of stress from the working stress they've been used to.' He believes we may have to revise radically our 1980s idea of stress as a high-status, 'executive' disease. In doing so we may come to realize, as Winston Churchill apparently said, that 'Work is a joy' and its lack an affliction. (As long as it's the right sort of work for the person in question, the occupational testers and psychometric counsellors are quick to point out.)

Overwork, for all its potential for harm, was not, like sloth, one of the Seven Deadly Sins. As Thomas Carlyle observed in the nineteenth century (and he lived to a ripe old age), 'Work is alone noble . . . A life of ease is not for any man.'

A recent survey released early in 1991 by the Industrial Society indicated that workaholism might not be as bad for the health of family life as was previously thought. Dedicated executives, it purported to prove, made *better* husbands and fathers than their less work-committed counterparts.

The *Daily Mail* reported, 'The most dedicated executives make the most devoted husbands and wives . . . Far from being grumpy or irritable when they get home, men and women who aim for the top at work usually treat their partners and children better than their lazier colleagues. And the hard-working bosses are more likely to be found digging the garden, painting the house or pushing a trolley around the supermarket at the weekend.' Jeremy Thorn, of the Industrial Society's consultancy services division, told the *Mail*, that 'Total quality is a way of life which extends beyond work to how you treat your husband, wife or children. You don't leave it behind when you drive out of the company car park.'

Laugh if you like, but leading matrimonial lawyer Peter Grose-Hodge, president of the élite International Academy of Matrimonial Lawyers, agrees. 'I don't believe overwork destroys marriages,' says the man who has seen more destroyed marriages than most men have had hot dinners. 'What splits the marriage is the unreasonable allocation of time *after* work – so that the wife is resentful that the husband spends the half-day he has playing golf rather than being with her and the children.' The only time the workload itself is likely to break up a marriage, in Grose-Hodge's experience, 'is when a great deal of work is not accompanied by a lot of money, and things around the house need doing and the man is never there to do them. Or, of course, if the work is being used as an excuse for something else.'

Grose-Hodge would even go so far as to say that 'workaholism can be a prophylactic *against* divorce, since men can retreat into their work to avoid quarrelling with their wives or splitting the family. That is why the divorce rate rises so sharply after the Christmas and summer holidays.'

Yet Hugh Jenkins, director of the Institute for Family Therapy, and Dr David Weeks, of the Royal Edinburgh Infirmary, will both testify to having attempted to patch up the ragged shreds that remain of the family lives of some workaholics, and Dr Weeks (himself also one, of course) calls workaholics 'the common cold of counselling' because he claims to see so many of them.

But Mr Jenkins and Dr Weeks agree that it is vital to distinguish between the work enthusiast, enhanced and invigorated by their occupation, and the dazed and dreary drudge, whose work engulfs and under-mines them. If you work so hard it keeps you from doing the things or being with the people you love, then you could be heading for health problems. But if you love your work so much that you cannot distinguish between it and having fun – and involve the people you love in it – you could have some advantages, in health terms, over those who work simply to earn a living.

As Dr Malcolm Carruther's wife and partner in workaholism, the psychologist Dr Vera Diamond, once observed, 'There's the creative workaholic and the kind that's desperately *driven* and running away from some other void in their lives. It's only the driven

ones who become ill.' But it is also often the driven
ones who are the most creative, and great creative
works have often come from great pain, like the
poetry of Sylvia Plath, or as a compensation for some
other loss, like Beethoven's Ninth Symphony.

Just as there is a world of difference between the
person who overeats out of a joyous appreciation of
good food and the compulsive 'binge' eater, who
gorges in secret and secretly despises the destructive
pattern of behaviour they feel powerless to prevent,
so it is important to distinguish between the
workaholic who thrives on an over-rich diet of work
and one who feels over-extended by a surfeit of it.

At the time of writing Professor Janet Spence of the
University of Texas, Austin, is at what she calls 'the
beginning' of a major psychological study of what
differentiates the work enthusiast from the workaholic. She has drawn up what she sees as 'three
defining characteristics', which, in her own words,
are:

1 Heavy psychological investment in work.
2 Degree of enjoyment: 'my work is more like fun'.
3 Degree of drivenness: 'the guilt factor – I feel as if
   I have to work whether I want to or not; I feel
   guilty when I don't work – there is something
   within me that compels me to work.'

What she calls a workaholic is 'high in work
investment, low in enjoyment and highly driven'. A
work enthusiast is 'equally invested but high in
enjoyment and low in driven'. Or, she agrees –
chewing over the idea when I put it to her – that a
work enthusiast might be driven by a *carrot* rather

than a stick, and that the carrot was not likely to be money. 'Both types tend to be attracted to "open-ended" jobs, where the number of hours you work and how much you put in is up to you,' she says.

'Blue-collar workaholics with set hours may go home and get involved in other projects, and if a person is workaholic and their job doesn't offer the investment they need, then they will find another outlet, paid or unpaid.'

What is most interesting about Professor Spence's work, as I see it, is that she has discovered that *the same person can be both types of workaholic at the same and/or at different times*. 'Many different patterns emerged,' she told me – and was still mulling over them. When I asked her whether she was a workaholic, she said laconically, 'Sometimes I am, and sometimes I'm a work enthusiast.'

I was most relieved to hear that, as even the most exuberant work enthusiast has to admit that there are *some* aspects of work they don't always enjoy, or the odd moment when they'd rather be wiggling their toes in the sea or stretched out in the sun than hunched over a desk or being brilliant in the boardroom.

'We suspected that the workaholics would be under very hard stress and feel overwhelmed by their work while the work enthusiasts were not – and that turned out to be true,' says Professor Spence. 'The workaholic would exhibit a lot of somatic complaints compared with the work enthusiasts, who might be ill less often than people who weren't so invested in their work. One important question we must ask is whether the health complaints of the workaholics are just the generally neurotic or whether there are very hard

long-term implications, like are they more likely to
develop ulcers and have heart attacks? That is not
easy data to get.'

In her research so far there has been no significant
sex differentiation, but she has discovered that
workaholics of both sexes were 'more likely to be
perfectionists and less able to delegate'. She also
believes she will be able to prove – 'although that data
is very difficult to get' – that workaholics, by her
definition, are less productive than work enthusiasts
and less likely to be found in high-level jobs.

Admittedly many workaholics work to fill up empty
spaces in other areas of their lives – like the chief
executive who confessed to me that he had turned
into a workaholic because he found fulfilment in his
job which he wasn't getting elsewhere, and because he
had a sense of 'control' in his professional life that his
personal life lacked. Take Donald Trump, pastmaster
of the 'art of the deal', who admitted in his book of that
title, 'I have a need to prove myself.' One of his
biographers, Joel Reed, suggested, in *Donald Trump: The
Man, The Myth, The Scandal* (Masquerade Books, 1990):
'His main impetus in life may have come from the fear
that his father found him lacking in many respects,
favoring instead one or more of the other Trump
children.' Compulsive wheeler-dealers like Trump,
many of whom flourished in the 1980s and 'fell' at the
dawn of the 1990s, find it almost impossible to stop.
But if they are deriving genuine fulfilment from their
work, their health is unlikely to suffer and may even
benefit from such displacement activity.

There is a world of difference between someone like
the ex-British Rail chairman Sir Peter Parker (at the
time of writing chairman of three other companies),

who told the *Sunday Times* that he routinely worked
between fourteen and sixteen hours a day, 'because it
is the most tremendous fun', and the desperately
driven workaholic computer operator who came to Dr
Malcolm Carruthers for help when he began getting
'yellow sweats' at night.

'He has been working with computers for twenty-
five years, getting up at 4 am every morning to be in
his office in London by 7, doesn't get home until 10 or
10.30 at night, snatches a few hours' sleep and starts
all over again. His wife is a workaholic too and they
run about four or five different enterprises together,
but not surprisingly their sex life has given way – he
says his wife doesn't feel like it at four o'clock in the
morning – and he doesn't want to change anything.
He just wants something to keep him going. I think
he's incurable. The sign that you're coping well is that
you're enjoying it. When the fun-factor goes . . .'

When I visited that formidable centre, the United
States National Institute on Aging in Washington,
DC, early in 1990, where 'golden oldies' in glittering
tracksuits jogged by, it had recently released a study,
part of its multi-billion dollar research into the effects
of ageing and how to minimize them, which suggested
that staying in the 'rat race' was one of the best ways
to stay young.

As I reported in *The Times*, the Institute found
through studies on rodents that 'rats who stay in the
rat race live up to 50 per cent longer than those who
opt out in favour of a gluttonous, sedentary retirement. And the Institute believes that many of its
recent studies of rats can be applied to human beings.'

The Institute's spry, fit, sixty-eight-year-old
director, Dr Frank Williams, explained to me how the

results surprised those who had assumed that a steady decline was inevitable. 'Much of our previous research involving rats and mice had shown a steady decline in older ones as compared with young ones – and we accepted that as the norm. But the rats had been unstimulated and allowed to eat a lot, gain weight and become indolent as they grew older. Now that studies include rats on active programmes the rats show far fewer effects of ageing and live up to 50 per cent longer. The message seems to be that if rats in the rat race last longer, people who stay involved – not necessarily in the rat race but in the human race – will last longer.'

Bearing that in mind, together with the pressures of demographic change, which will mean many more old people by the end of the 1990s and a dwindling pool of people to support them, the elderly will increasingly be wooed back into the workforce, as some companies – supermarkets, DIY chains and even one famous fast-food organization – are already doing, with several prototype outlets boasting *only* staff over fifty. Whether such 'granny ghettoes' are a good idea remains to be seen, but it is undoubtedly good to give the active elderly an outlet for what W H Auden called the 'foiled creative fire' that, it is beginning to be thought, may convert itself into cancer and other diseases if it remains frustrated.

The workaholic culture reached such fever pitch in America in the 1980s that an organization calling itself 'Workaholics Anonymous' was founded in 1983 and is still in existence, with small groups meeting from coast to coast, operating on principles similar to those of Alcoholics Anonymous.

The management consultant Diane Fassel believes

that workaholism is a 'disease' which must be stamped out of any civilized society. An outspoken advocate of Workaholics Anonymous, it is her contention that workaholics – whom she likes to think of as 'work addicts' – are also likely to become addicted to other things, such as alcohol, food, money or 'relationships'. Her book *Working Ourselves to Death* (Harper & Row, 1990) puts forward this view, holding out little hope for the long-term health of the workaholic. Her 'deadly continuum' of workaholic health problems includes blackouts, chronic headaches, backaches, high blood pressure, ulcers, depression, strokes, serious illness, emotional deadness, moral and spiritual bankruptcy and death – all, admittedly, in the 'late stage' of the 'disease', but a pretty grim list nevertheless.

The only road to recovery, as she sees it, is for the workaholic to admit his or her 'powerlessness', accept that the urge to work is a 'disease' and 'actively seek help' – specifically from the 'Twelve-step Program' Workaholics Anonymous has adapted almost word for word from Alcoholics Anonymous. It was explained to me by one of the founder members, a 'recovered workaholic' who would give his name only as 'Dan' since anonymity is the essence of the organization.

'I'm alive, thank God. Some of us don't make it,' he told me with fervent gratitude. 'I had an uncle who *died* of workaholism.' 'Dan' had, he explained, been a financial analyst for a large corporation until the pressure became too much for him and he decided 'to get out of management'. His work had been his 'mistress', he said with considerable distaste. Now he apparently has time to appreciate his wife and nineteen-year-old son, in addition to running

Workaholics Anonymous, albeit in a laid-back sort of way. As he explained to me, 'We're doing some brochures but it'll be a while before we finish them because, as you can understand, we don't work under too much pressure here.'

The Twelve-step Program – also propounded by Fassel – requires:

1 Admitting you are 'powerless' over 'compulsive working' and that your life has become unmanageable.
2 Coming to believe that a 'power greater than yourself could restore you to sanity'.
3 Making a decision to turn your will and your life over to the care of God (or any great power in which you believe).
4 Making a 'searching and fearless moral inventory of ourselves'.
5 Admitting 'to God, to ourselves, and to another human being the exact nature of our wrongs'.
6 Being 'entirely ready to have God remove all these defects of character'.
7 'Humbly' asking 'Him to remove our shortcomings'.
8 Making a list of all persons you have harmed and becoming willing to make amends to them all.
9 Making direct amends to such people wherever possible.
10 Continuing to take a personal inventory.
11 Seeking through prayer and meditation to improve conscious contact with God . . . praying for the knowledge of His will for you.
12 Having had a spiritual awakening as a result of these steps, trying to carry this message to other workaholics and to practise these principles.

None of this seems to relate very well to the glowing work enthusiasts I have quoted in earlier chapters, who would, I am sure, have little desire to become cringingly contrite converts to this new religion of dependency. There might be some weary drones who would appreciate an opportunity to slow down their treadmills and swear allegiance, but then, there were probably some people who thought the Stepford Wives – those zombie-like creations who were supposed to be the perfect little middle-American housewives in the Bryan Forbes film of the same name – would make the ideal mate!

Much of what Fassel and her co-author of the book *The Addictive Organization* (Harper & Row, 1988), Anne Wilson Schaef, say has validity for the 'driven' workaholic, and their campaign against 'unrealistic expectations, impossible job descriptions and a corporate culture that pursues profit above everything else' is to be applauded. Yet their work – at least what I have read of it – largely ignores the contribution of the creative workaholic, who may be addicted to work but is on a perpetual high, with no desire to come down. I am more interested in distinguishing what differentiates the health of the dynamos from that of the drones – the creative work enthusiast and the automaton undeniably on automatic pilot towards self-destruct.

Towards the end of the 1980s experts working in different areas of health and stress research were beginning to evolve a similar theory to explain why some people seemed to thrive on an inhuman workload while others collapsed from much less – although they reached their conclusions in different ways and used varying terminologies to describe their findings. The idea they were all groping towards was basically that it's not *what* you do or even how *much* you do but how you *perceive* what you do that most affects your health. A picture began to emerge of the so-called 'hardy personality', who regarded potential threats as challenges, and relished those challenges. My totally unscientific hunch is that it is into such a category that most true work enthusiasts fall.

The basis of the 'hardy personality' – or the Type C personality, if you like (to distinguish it from aggressive, time-urgent Type As, slower-moving, less 'driven' Type Bs, and what Dr David Lewis calls Type Hs for haste, hostility and a proneness to heart attacks) is 'conviction, challenge and control': a *conviction* in themselves, the ability to regard what lesser mortals might see as threats as *challenges* and at least the *delusion* of being in *control*.

My findings for a feature I did for the *Sunday Express Magazine* in 1990 on 'the healing power of power' seemed to bear this out. So-called 'executive stress' symptoms such as ulcers and hypertension, I discovered, were more likely to be provoked by a sense of powerlessness than one of responsibility. 'When people have "made it" and feel secure, their stress hormones actually drop,' Dr Carruthers's research had shown. So, apparently, does their need of sleep. American researchers at the National Bureau of Economic Research at the University of Michigan recently discovered that the more successful people are, the less sleep they need. Professor Cooper's research confirmed, 'It's the middle managers, or those without a real sense of power and control, who seem to suffer more from stress-related diseases than those at the top.'

Blood pressure, for example, usually rises with stress. Yet world leaders are supposedly under constant stress and – at least according to Edwina Currie, in her book *Life Lines* (Sidgwick & Jackson, 1989) – Margaret Thatcher used to marvel at the low blood pressure she and her counterparts around the summit tables apparently professed – to each other – to maintain.

Whether this is true or not cannot be confirmed, but Dr Carruthers suggested it might be so because people who are in high-pressure positions that they are suited for find ways of adapting to survive them. Chief among these strategies is the ability to convert apparent threats – which raise the blood's level of the fight-or-flight hormone adrenaline – to challenges – which produce a surge of the more productive hormone noradrenaline to induce positive feelings rather than panic.

Producing too much of the former can have an adverse affect on the health, whereas the latter may actually enhance it, giving the work enthusiast a noradrenaline 'high', similar to the kick exercise addicts achieve from the endorphins – opiate-like chemicals – produced by their brains.

There is a growing conjecture that the 'hardy personality' is more resistant to disease than the rest of us.

The 'futurist' Christine McNulty believes that those she calls 'the leading-edge people' – the 'inner-directeds' who do what they do out of conviction and commitment rather than in the pursuit of personal gain – 'are sick much less than other types of workers'. She attributes this to a phenomenon known as 'psychoneuroimmunology', and notes that 'while people are being taught to control their immune systems through what is known as psychoneuro-immunology in the United States, we believe that these "leading edge" people do it instinctively, and that is very exciting.'

You can be a 'leading edger' even if you're not in what you consider an earth-shattering job, and you can work on developing the knack of psychoneuro-immunology even while doing seemingly mindless tasks, such as photocopying or stuffing envelopes, if you do them in the right frame of mind. As Heather Tilbury – who began by collating telephone directories for 2s 6d – says, 'Nothing need ever be wasted – even stuffing envelopes at midnight. It depends on how you think of it. When I was collating telephone directories, I used to make up mind-games as I was doing it, and you can always do exercises to strengthen your tummy muscles or derive some benefit from any activity, however boring, if you think positively. I once wrote an article on "How to improve your sex life at the bus stop" – if you get my drift!'

Secretaries and clerical assistants should not think they are there simply to take orders but should use their initiative to take control, one secretarial agency head tells all her staff – whether that means attempting to initiate a radical change in office policy or introducing a new type of petty-cash book. 'You can acquire a sense of control which brings with it a sense of job satisfaction whatever job you do,' this shrewd mentor advises. 'And people who have that sense of satisfaction are less likely to lose working days due to sickness,' she has discovered.

Many of the tricks she teaches are things a workaholic does instinctively.

Diane Fassel argues, 'Workaholics love crisis and they precipitate crisis . . . it is another form of an adrenaline high.' Certainly the acknowledged work-aholic Margaret Thatcher seemed to thrive on crises, and often likened herself to the great wartime leader Churchill, who seemed to share the philosophy of his contemporary Franklin Delano Roosevelt, America's longest-serving president, that, 'There is nothing I love as much as a good fight.'

Admittedly there is a danger that the Dunkirk-spirited workaholic will become so addicted to the thrill of constant challenges that, like the drug addict or the dangerous-sport enthusiast, he or she will require an increasingly large 'hit' to reach the requisite level for optimum performance.

Margaret Thatcher's stirring speeches during the no-confidence debate that followed her resignation, were a prime example of peak performance under duress. Her defiant assertion that she was 'enjoying' herself on what should have been the most stressful day of her political career was an example of the euphoric buzz that 'eustress' or creative stress, as the psychologist Dr David Lewis calls it, can bring.

Dr Lewis holds corporate workshops in 'creative stress'. His theory is that stress should not be eliminated from our lives (or we would *all* go around like Stepford Wives), but that we should learn to recognize our optimum stress levels and how to achieve them without going over the top and into the danger zone.

He stresses, though, that everyone's levels are different. 'Certain people need a good deal of stress to spur them on to their best efforts – such as an actress who may require a degree of stage fright in order to

give the performance of her life. If I were to try to
make these people generally more relaxed, I might
make them less good at their job,' says Lewis – who
nevertheless teaches relaxation techniques 'so that
they can learn to relax when they are not working so
that they can spend their – finite – amount of "stress
currency" to best advantage.'

I know that I can tell in myself when I am working
on a spurt of positive, 'creative' stress, and when I am
experiencing a spiral of negative stress which is totally
unconstructive. With the former I feel as if I am firing
on all cylinders. Perhaps I've just telephoned a
newspaper with an idea for a feature and the editor
says, 'Great, can you do it so that we can publish it
tomorrow?' Everything in my workaholic soul rises to
the challenge, I can feel the noradrenaline surge and
my mind switches into fast gear. Potential diversions
are ignored with iron discipline, and all my energies
are focused on the task at hand. Somehow everyone I
need is there, as if by magic, when I telephone; the
research I request is faxed exactly when I need it to
confirm my theory; and, as they used to say in *The
A-Team*, 'Don't you just love it when a plan comes
together?' When I finish – always in the nick of time –
there is a supreme sense of satisfaction and accomplishment. Only then I may realize that I haven't had
anything to eat, or been to the toilet, all day, that
there's nothing in the house for dinner and that I'd
foolishly promised to bake a cake for the school fair
the next day.

At other times, under what is technically, I suppose,
far *less* stress, I can feel things getting on top of me –
and it's usually *not* my work. Maybe the house is a
mess, there are bills which need querying as well as

paying, the car tax has run out, there are letters which require lengthy answers, a leak in the roof which is becoming insistently evident, a complicated dish to prepare for dinner guests I'm beginning to wish I hadn't invited, guilty reminders of maternal duties not performed. Everything seems to be crowding in on me even *before* the magazine editor telephones to ask if I could please immediately update the article on Christmas gifts I did the year before and have completely forgotten. If the fight-or-flight hormone adrenaline is being released, it invokes an urge to flee from the whole mess and a sense of being tired of having to fight it all. The effect is debilitating and a complete contrast to the exhilaration of the earlier scenario.

The most significant difference is in the sense of being in *control*. This sense of control – real or illusory – is now considered crucial not only to the productivity but to the health and psychological well-being of a workforce. Indeed, cancer is thought by some psychologists to be a tangible symptom of the sense of losing control of life.

Looking back at the beginning of 1990 over the occupational stress 'league tables' he did for the *Sunday Times* in 1984, Professor Cary Cooper noted, 'The link between the high-stress jobs was not just a high workload but change and lack of control.' Uncertainty about the industry – as with miners at the time – and enforced relocation were other stress factors. As a general rule of thumb, Cooper found, 'The higher the *perception of autonomy*, the lower the stress level and therefore the stress-related illnesses experienced by the workers in that job.' . . . 'If I was redoing those tables today,' he told me for a feature I was writing on stress for *The Times*, 'teachers would move up from very stressful to extremely stressful.' Doctors, who were given a 6.8, 'two-star' stress rating in 1984, would move up the scale substantially, he felt, after the White Paper on reorganization, which meant that they had to worry more about paperwork and administration.

How workers' expectations of their jobs matched up with reality was an important factor in determining stress levels too, so that the armed forces and merchant navy ranked comparatively low on the tables compared with the police force and prison service, which people might join idealistically, unprepared for the harsher realities and constraints of the job, Professor Cooper speculated.

He also suggested that the single European market of 1992 would bring increasing stresses for all of Britain. 'On top of all the travel and relocation and mergers and new methods to cope with the European Community, British business will perceive itself to be losing control to bureaucrats in Brussels. As a whole country we'll be losing control!'

Since producing the tables Professor Cooper and his team went on to do more detailed studies on large groups of commercial pilots, doctors, City dealers, teachers, tax officers, air traffic controllers and civil service mandarins. These studies involved blood chemistry tests as well as asking participants to fill out comprehensive questionnaires about their jobs, life styles and aspirations.

Blood samples taken from teachers, for example, just after the summer holidays were compared with those taken just before Christmas, and Cooper was confident that he would find a discernible difference in cholesterol, fibrinogen and other 'stress markers', which, he explained, rose in both sexes when they were under stress.

Professor Cooper has, as yet, done no study of the self-employed, who, he predicted, will become an increasingly significant proportion of the working population in the 1990s, but he suspects that their sense of autonomy might cancel out a good deal of their stress. And he recommends conscious 'coping strategies', such as will be outlined in Chapter 7, to minimize the stress all work is heir to.

Dr Thomas Stuttaford began an article on stress in *The Times* by pointing out: 'The Bible exhorts us to labour hard in this world, for there is no work in the grave. It doesn't explain if this is a promise or a threat, and disregards the possibility that working hard with thy might, as advocated in Ecclesiastes, might bring the day of reckoning nearer.'

He then went on to describe the symptoms of stress, pointing out that: 'signs and symptoms that somebody is failing to cope with work stress often first become apparent at home, where the once placid breadwinner may verbally, or even physically, lash out at his wife and children. He will become isolated by his anxieties so that small problems become obsessions. The once strong man will weaken, may even become tearful, will find it difficult to get to sleep and may wake in the early hours to worry over his competence. Drinking habits change; the social drinker shuns companions and may therefore drink less, whereas the home-lover, normally abstemious, may take to the bottle. With the irritability goes the loss of self-confidence, so that thoughts lose their directions and decisions are delayed: the hallmark of stress is change in personality rather than any individual symptom.'

Unexplained backaches, headaches and a sense of general malaise can dog the unhappy worker – and, indeed, if any of these symptoms or the ones above are a chronic component of your life, then they may well be a sign to slow down, or at least change direction.

As the Canadian Dr Peter Hanson observed in his book *The Joy of Stress* (Pan, 1987), 'Lack of satisfaction on the job breeds discontent, lowered self-image, brooding, moody behaviour and often increased arguments at home with the family . . . Dr Laurence Peter, author of *The Peter Principle*, has demonstrated that it is all too common for people in a job hierarchy to continue to be promoted until they reach their level of incompetence. The corollary of this is that, in any hierarchy, each person tends to rise until he or she becomes incompetent at a job. It is at that level that he or she stays, being considered unsuitable for further promotion. (If this is commonly true, the majority of jobs are held by incompetents.)' He advises not being afraid to say 'no' if you think you are being promoted in the wrong direction, or to ask for your old job back if you start experiencing some of the unpleasant symptoms of stress without any of the buzz of achievement.

A workaholic who habitually neglects his family and friends for work, Dr Hanson warns, and doesn't even take the time to walk the dog or stroke the cat, 'could be gravely weakening . . . stress resistance as well as shortening . . . life', since they are a valuable 'safety net' or buffer against stress. He advises frequent physical touching – of people and of pets – for longevity, a recommendation which is reinforced by the results of some of the rat tests done by the United

States National Institute on Aging.

Even genuine work enthusiasts who adore their jobs can sometimes experience 'off' periods in which work-related stresses can pile up. When I interviewed the usually sparkling Susan Hampshire one day backstage in her Birmingham dressing-room in the middle of the gruelling tour of *The King and I*, which had kept her away from her home for the better part of four months at a time, she was looking slightly strained and admitted that – just at that moment – she was so tired her mind felt as 'unfocused' as a dyslexic's vision of the alphabet. Yet she explained to me how she used the power of positive thinking – assisted by acupuncture and some homoeopathic constitutionals – to keep her voice strong, and had (so far) successfully avoided the colds and throat infections that had dogged the rest of the cast. And the actor Donald Sinden recently enthused to *The Times*: 'I'm not incredibly healthy – I'm an actor. Actors don't believe in illness, so we don't get ill. The curtain goes up and it doesn't matter how you're feeling, you're on . . . You can cure most things by the power of the mind. It has to be mind over matter because when the curtain goes up you've got to be there, you have to talk yourself into being all right.'

People in positions of power are as aware as actors and athletes of the power of positive thinking. Crack the concentration of a top tennis or snooker player and they've lost the match, no matter how technically skilled they may be, and there is ample anecdotal evidence that a belief in your own invincibility is about the closest you can come to achieving that sought-after state. Inner-directed work enthusiasts tend to have such a belief instinctively and, as Christine

McNulty believes, benefit greatly from it.

Everyone marvelled at how Margaret Thatcher – a woman more imbued than most with a sense of invincibility – appeared to grow more youthful and vigorous each year of her eleven-and-a-half-year reign – with the exception of those brief periods when her supremacy was seriously threatened.

There were signs that the Iron Lady could suffer from metal fatigue when a chink in her armour was found. As I pointed out in the *Sunday Express Magazine* feature on power and health during the personal attacks that followed the sinking of the *Belgrano* (1982) and the Westland affair (1985–6), she suffered a series of minor illnesses and operations. There was a detached retina in 1983, the Depuytrens contracture of the hand, which was corrected in 1986, and during the same period she is reported to have experienced neck and shoulder pains which caused her to resort to aromatherapy massages and electrified baths; and she even apparently fainted once at a Buckingham Palace reception. Coincidences? Perhaps, or maybe these were threats she could somehow not manage to twist into constructive challenges. Even the most adroit at doing so can suffer occasional lapses.

Since Mrs Thatcher's well-being seemed so linked with the state of her standing in the nation, it was natural for worries to be expressed about her health when she was forced – so prematurely, from her perspective – to give up the prime ministership, and I expect to see her age much more swiftly than she would have had she been allowed to go 'on and on' in office.

The Greek President Andreas Papandreou's heart trouble flared when his popularity waned, and the health of the deposed Philippines President Ferdinand Marcos quickly declined in exile.

Dr Lewis suggested that Mrs Thatcher had better find an important new role to play quickly, or her health might suffer as a consequence of an unwished-for early retirement. He likened her – somewhat ungallantly – to 'an old fridge that has chugged on perfectly well until it is moved, when it may fall apart'.

In a surprisingly frank and poignant interview, Mrs Thatcher told *Vanity Fair* that when she had been so summarily 'bundled out' of Downing Street, 'the pattern of my life was fractured. It is like throwing a pane of glass with a complicated map upon it on the floor, and all the habits and thoughts and actions that went with it . . . you could not pick up those pieces.' Sometimes she could no longer remember what day it was, she lamented.

Work enthusiasts who are made to retire reluctantly
at an arbitrary date can suffer serious health
consequences, just like those who are obliged to stay
on at work unwillingly. Especially those to whom, like
Mrs Thatcher, 'home is where you come to when you
have nothing better to do'. But the health of non-
workaholics may actually improve after retirement.
Just look at how the American President Jimmy
Carter appeared to age twenty years during his
dispiriting term at the White House, when he must
have suffered acutely from feelings of powerlessness
over the hostage crisis which humiliated his administration. He looked years younger when the weight of
office was lifted from his shoulders. So did Gerald
Ford, an unelected caretaker who had never sought
the absolute power of the presidency. Uneasy heads
should clearly *not* wear the crown.

But people who are happy in their working 'skins',
who feel that their job fits them – neither too big nor
too small but just right – and offers the right levels of
challenge and satisfaction, and a sense of success and
achievement, are likely to be healthier than those with
the sense of running on a treadmill just to try and keep
up – or twiddling their thumbs while dreaming of
early retirement. And although workaholism *can* be a
tragic treadmill it can also be a magic roundabout, a
transport of delight that doesn't *have* to spin in a
vicious circle.

6

Deadlier Than the Male?

*'Man may work from sun to sun
But women's work is never done.'*

Anon

*'This above all: to thine own self be true,
And it must follow, as the night the day,
Thou canst not then be false to any man.'*

William Shakespeare

A brilliant British businesswoman who is chairman and chief executive, as well as owning a controlling stake in a company in a highly competitive international field, told me she had to make sure always to be home before her partner because he couldn't stand coming home to a dark, cold, lonely house.

For a true work enthusiast like this woman, who had not scheduled children into her life, this obviously added considerable pressure to what must already have been an extremely high-pressure day. The live-in boyfriend – himself managing director of a company – would, she insisted, rather drive around aimlessly (and increasingly irritatedly) until she got home than go in, light the fire and start the dinner himself.

Bizarre though this ritual sounds, it is not some isolated neurosis that this particular couple needs to work out. Other women will no doubt nod understandingly. Their partners may not attempt to exercise droit de seigneur over their working lives in quite the same way, but they will, most probably, intrude upon or undermine the women's work enthusiasm somehow – however unconsciously or unintentionally. (Excuse me while I break off to fix my husband's breakfast!).

Many working women – particularly those with challenging, high-powered careers – cite similar phenomena, and this syndrome was pinpointed in the perceptive book on the 'backlash' that can occur in dual career marriages, *Successful Women, Angry Men*, by the American author Bebe Moore Campbell (Arrow Books, 1988).

As Ms Campbell shrewdly observed, 'Most men don't have a problem with their wives working late; but it is hard for them to feel manly when they come into an empty house. Their fathers came home to a smiling, encouraging wife who had dinner ready – and that is part of what defined them as "Daddy".'

These women's partners, she went on to say, were not *really* being as petty and male chauvinist piggish as they seemed. 'Their husbands may seem to be asking them to cook and clean, but they are really asking for help in finding a new way to feel masculine. They are seeking the same kind of wholeness that women are after,' she opined.

All very well and good, and probably quite true. But it doesn't make things any easier for the women work enthusiasts who have to cope with the backlash in this transitional period. After you've been banging your head against the 'glass ceiling' all day at the office, you shouldn't have to come home and bash the pots and pans about and bung the baby in the bath. But that's what many working women – workaholic or not – have to do. As *Fortune* magazine discovered, 'Even in two-career families, women handle about 70 per cent of the child-rearing.' It is this double burden which may drain and dispirit her even if she is uplifted by her work.

Helen (Lady) Ward, a highly successful solicitor who is married to a judge and the mother of six-year-old twin daughters never seems the least bit drained or dispirited – but, she points out, she accomplishes what she does only with a tremendous amount of effort and organization and a minimal amount of sleep, and she gets irritated by articles on working mothers that make it all look so easy. Her words articulately encapsulate the situation in which so many women work enthusiasts with demanding careers and family demands find themselves.

'I take my responsibility to my clients very seriously and in order to work satisfactorily to the level I do, I work three or four nights a week until three or four in the morning. I can go to bed at 4.15 and still get up at 6 or 7 the next morning – although on Saturdays I collapse,' she told me. 'I work so late so that I can get home at a reasonable time to cook the children dinner, read to them, watch the news with my husband, smile, and start working again at 10 o'clock. The other three nights I work until 1 or sometimes 2 am. If I ever break the routine and go out to dinner, I feel completely shattered!

'Because my husband's on the bench, he doesn't get much work to do at home and he gets very fed up about it sometimes, but I think he remembers what it was like when he was a busy Silk. There's only certain things one can delegate. I take my children to school, so I don't start work until 9.30, whereas a lot of my partners are here at 8 o'clock. But it's terribly tough.

'It's terribly tough to be good-humoured and concentrate on small children when you're exhausted and find an overwhelming amount of work waiting for you, and terribly difficult to concentrate on one's partners at times. I can tell I sometimes have this glazed look on my face with clients because I'm realizing I've forgotten to phone the butcher – and I don't think such a thought ever crosses a man's mind!

'I try to cut myself into pieces, because I believe most women have to be multi-faceted in a way men don't have to be. How many women have you heard who say they think they've got Alzheimer's Disease since they had children, and that they *had* to wander out and buy the nearest Armani because they hadn't the time to wander around and look for something several thousand pounds cheaper!' She clearly hasn't lost her sense of humour.

There have been women workaholics since long before women were allowed to work, and busy home-makers who bustle about baking bread, knitting sweaters, making jam for the church fête, running charity events and dabbling in interior decoration may be included in the species. As much as working women, Anne Wilson Schaef targets them in her *Meditations for Women Who Do Too Much*, with its daily pearls of wisdom from well-known women. For example, 'At work, you think of the children you have left at home. At home, you think of the work you've left unfinished. Such a struggle is unleashed within yourself, your heart is rent' (Golda Meir); 'Integrity is so perishable in the summer months of success' (Vanessa Redgrave); 'Make it a rule of life never to regret and never look back. Regret is an appalling waste of energy; you can't build on it; it is good only for wallowing in' (Katherine Mansfield).

In the 1980s, when more women were allowed – even encouraged – to be workaholic *outside the home* than ever before, it was noticeable how many men divorced their youthful loves of the 1960s and 1970s, who had metamorphosed into the assertive career women of the 1980s. In subsequent marriages, they sought a more nurturing home-maker figure of the kind their fathers had married in the 1940s and 1950s. Interestingly too, the power-suited, minimalist mothers had spawned a generation of ultra-feminine 'pink and frilly' daughters, who appeared to be rejecting their mothers' workaholic ethic. And a leading sociologist, Dr Eleanor Macdonald, told a recruitment conference in 1991: 'In England we have a generation of women whose sole interest is boys and lipsticks', being left behind by ambitious European career women.

The backlash against working women (in addition to sheer lust) could help to explain the large number of thirty- and forty-something men remarrying women many years younger than themselves, who were prepared to feed their egos as well as their faces while producing 'designer' babies and turning out attractively at corporate functions. And why – as *New York* magazine recently noted – so many executive women in their thirties and forties are turning to younger men who had been raised with different expectations and, perhaps, were more accustomed to coming home to empty houses.

As the president of the Manhattan Borough Bank, Ruth Messenger (fifty years old and married to Andrew Lachman, a forty-three-year-old school administrator), explained, 'My being a public figure is not a problem. Andrew is sure enough of himself that he takes pleasure in what I do without being threatened.'

Janet Street-Porter, head of the BBC's 'youth programming' and forty-four at the time of writing, told the *Sunday Express Magazine*'s 'Out to Lunch' column that she was going out with a twenty-four-year-old photographer and youth television presenter after three failed marriages, including one to *Time Out* publisher Tony Elliott, whom she described as 'exactly the same age, a workaholic like me . . . I was an outsider, striving to get on in a magazine world dominated by Sloanes,' the unconventional Street-Porter recalled. 'I wasn't very nice in those days and it was difficult when Tony went through the transitional phase between being someone who started a business on his mother's dining-room table to becoming a millionaire.'

Reading between the lines it sounds as if she was saying that she was too busy with her own workaholic aspirations to give him the support which male workaholics have come to expect but female ones have learned to do without. And it seems in keeping with the new mood for talented career women of the 1980s to enthuse about how they have made their husbands their prime priorities for the 1990s. On successive days this year there were reports of tennis player Chris Evert saying, 'When I was with Jimmy Connors and John Lloyd, my sport came first. Now my marriage is my top priority', and violinist Anne-Sophie Mutter, considered by many to be the greatest in the world, putting her career on hold to be with her husband for a while. 'I devoted myself to the violin from childhood because I wanted to,' she told one newspaper. 'My violin is the best part of my body, it is an extension of my soul and heart.' But she was looking forward to 'developing other interests and doing things I don't normally have time to do'. Most of all, she said, she wanted 'to be a wife to my husband'.

Peter Grose-Hodge, often called 'the solicitor for husbands', because his sympathies seem to lie with them although he maintains he acts for more women than men, believes the reason so many two-career marriages are breaking up is that 'Anybody who does a hard day's work needs a wife to look after him or her, and unless they have made proper logistic arrangements the marriage will fail.' Men who married the girl next door and then moved to a posher house and a better standard of living often left their childhood sweethearts behind and were 'bowled over', as Grose-Hodge puts it, by the *soignée*, sophisticated career women they suddenly found themselves working with. But they soon tired of microwaving their own meals.

As Bebe Moore Campbell wrote, 'Baby boomers became enmeshed in corporations and they found themselves trapped in a work life that included the late hours, travel and after-hours socializing that is standard in most companies. Home life was often a boring routine with husbands and wives in a state of near collapse and neither receiving the nurturance they needed. Couples were forced to direct their energies towards constant preparation for the next day's work rather than towards each other.'

According to a survey in *GQ* (Gentleman's Quarterly) magazine released in 1991, of 1,000 men aged between twenty-five and forty-five and earning over £25,000 a year, the 'New Man' who promised to care *and* share doesn't exist (surprise, surprise) – which explains why women workaholics are doubly handicapped. Of the married men surveyed, 65 per cent felt they should be the breadwinner and expected all the support systems to go with their status.

It is a truth still almost universally acknowledged that a single man in want of more than a middle-management position must also be in possession of a wife, and it is no coincidence, the British Institute of Management told me for an article in *The Times* in 1988, that of the nearly 3,000 top British executives who participated in its 'Profile of British Industry' survey that year, 81 per cent were married and only 12 per cent single and 7 per cent divorced or separated and not remarried. The statistics I saw were not 'broken down by sex and age', as the saying goes (although many of the managers, no doubt, were), but I would suspect that a disproportionately high number within the single and divorced categories were women – if there were any women surveyed.

Leah Hertz, in her book *The Business Amazons* (André Deutsch, 1986) found that 51.4 per cent of female executives and 37 per cent of female business owners were 'unattached', whereas 93.5 per cent of male executives were married. This was a clear indication, as she saw it, of how difficult women found it to combine marriage, let alone motherhood, with top careers in companies in which it was necessary to put in the long, set hours that the workaholic work ethic of the 1980s demanded. And if they could put in the working hours, they had few to spare for the work-orientated socializing which was *de rigueur* for getting ahead in the corporate culture.

Corporate woman, according to Hertz (herself an entrepreneur who founded – with her husband – the fashion firm Crochetta) was the one with the blank space on her executive desk where the picture of wife and kids usually went. And even if she *has* managed to acquire and hold on to a husband and family, she is wary of showing their photographs. As the equal opportunities consultant Ivy Cameron told the *Daily Mail* in 1991, 'If a woman executive has photographs of her children, she is seen as a soft worker who puts her babies first.' (Hopefully the photographs of female soldiers in the Gulf with pictures of the babies they'd left behind defiantly displayed on their helmets will have done something to debunk that old wives' tale.)

'Unlike male executives, women executives and

owners do not have the same motivation to get married,' Hertz pointed out, 'because for them marriage is not going to provide the good-looking, caring, listening, cooking wife that the businessman gets in exchange for his financial support. What marriage has to offer them is usually a demanding husband who has to be pampered after a long day at work.'

Childcare is still – unfairly – considered the woman's responsibility, whether it comes out of her (taxed) income or is left to her to coordinate via an intricate network of relatives and friends. Company crèches, however good an idea they seem to the childless career woman determined to 'have it all', and although they have received some support from the government in the form of tax concessions, are usually inadequate for any more than a first child up to the age of two or three. And even if the mother can afford a nanny to ferry her offspring to playgroups and doctor's appointments and parties, she will usually have to concern herself with the coordination of these efforts in a way male workaholics do not.

It will be a long time, I fear, before company crèches are considered a unisex facility – and 'paternity leave', pioneered as long as a decade ago by enlightened companies such as Penguin Books, is still largely a subject of mirth.

So women workaholics, particularly those with children to consider, may find it easier to work at home, or at least to be their own bosses. For many women – who are allowed the 'luxury' of working only so long as they can continue to take care of the supposed feminine necessities such as shopping, cooking, cleaning and childcare – working from home, or as their own boss, is the *only* way they can manage to work with commitment and without having to watch the clock. One self-employed executive I know keeps her baby, for the time being, in a cradle by her desk in the office, rocking it while she runs her business if not quite ruling the world. Another, working from home, has rigged up a play zone for her toddler in a corner of the room she uses as an office. Tapes of 'office sounds' are now on sale for home-workers in just such situations who want to sound more professional on the telephone!

The government minister Angela Rumbold, MP, is one of many progressive employers who has shown by example what is possible. Her own daughter, she told me with pride, served most professionally as her Parliamentary Private Secretary, working primarily from home with her baby playing contentedly (well, most of the time) at her feet.

While for non-workaholics home-working is fraught with pitfalls – there is a constant round of interruptions, innumerable household tasks and callers crying out for attention, and unlimited opportunity to skive – the workaholic home-worker will happily allow the working day to expand into night, and can continue working after the children are in bed and before making breakfast and hope no one will notice as they would if she were working late at an office.

Susan Hampshire told me how she discovered she could write late at night and in the wee hours of the morning. Lizzie Webb would take a break after school to see the son she missed when she went off before dawn to her early-morning television slot – and then made use of evenings after her son was in bed to work out her exercise routines and write her books.

Male workaholics can be more open about their preoccupation, since a man is expected to occupy himself with earning a living. But a woman may have to learn cunning tricks to avoid accusations of workaholism, hiding her enthusiasm as alcoholics do their bottle – not because she feels ashamed of it but because she is made to feel, by others, that such enthusiasm is unfeminine if not downright unnatural.

A woman workaholic is regarded (sometimes by both her mate and the men she works with) as an aberration who has gone against nature and nurture. Her spouse is likely to resent her commitment to work – either because he does not share it or because it stops her from devoting herself more slavishly to him. Or he may be jealous of the prestige, power and pay packet her workaholic efforts bring – so that she, like so many women, must become what I think of as an 'invisible earner', one who minimizes her success and status in order to appease her mate. (Bebe Moore Campbell's *Successful Women, Angry Men* affords many examples of such relationships.)

So frequently it is not a woman's *work* that is the strain but how to juggle it to accommodate the household chores, the child-rearing and all the domestic duties to which men are so often impervious (which could explain why so many leading entre-preneurs, in a survey in 1991, cited their mother as being the spur to their success).

If women workaholics burn out quicker than men – as Dr Malcolm Carruthers has found – despite their better ability to cope with workplace stress than their male counterparts (Professor Cooper's findings), it is probably due to the strain of their multiple roles. You can give the family fast food, but male egos, it seems, still require feeding in the old-fashioned way.

Those who are not bound by office hours or conventions can often accomplish much more by taking time off when they feel like it and working at ridiculous hours, but it may become difficult to draw a distinction between 'personal' and working life, particularly for women who, like Susan Hampshire and Lizzie Webb, not only love their work but work with the men they love. Women workaholics who have found it prudent to work with their mates are probably wise, for the shared enthusiasm for work can spill over into personal lives and therefore does not 'exclude' the partner. I am always suspicious of couples who work together, or in similar professions, and say sanctimoniously, 'We make it a rule never to talk business at home.' Why ever not, if they both enjoy doing so?

The inspirational work enthusiast Anita Roddick, whose Body Shop was one of the great business success stories of the 1980s, loved working with her husband, Gordon, so much that she encouraged other couples such as Jilly Forster and Rob Lamond to become part of her international team. So much of their sexual energy, she once told me, seemed to go into the business – to the mutual benefit of both the business and the sexuality. For the genuine work enthusiast work can be a turn-on. (Remember Sir Ralph 'five-times-a-night' Halpern?) It is only the mechanical drone, the unwilling workaholic, whose libido is lessened. But male workaholics undoubtedly find it easier to find people to wait up for them and hang adoringly on their arms at business functions.

Professor Cooper's research showed that elsewhere dual-career couples were – like the couple whose story began this chapter – getting tired of coming home to 'a cold house, an instant dinner and an equally tired and unsympathetic spouse'. But that is where being married to – or romantically involved with – someone in the same firm, even the same profession, can come in handy – a wizard wheeze many workaholics have already twigged. In America the end of the 1980s saw the beginning of a booming business in 'Lonelyhearts' columns in professional journals, with doctors, lawyers and stockbrokers wanting to meet 'like-minded' members of the opposite sex in the same profession.

The Aids scare, as the proponent of office romance mentioned earlier, Dr James Martin, found, contributed to a climate in which people were becoming frightened of meeting others outside the security of their own professions. The 'singles bars' which flourished in the 1970s were deserted.

If you're in the civil service it can be a relief to discuss matters you are forbidden to tell outsiders under the Official Secrets Act, a member of the service, who, naturally, wishes to remain anonymous, confessed. If you've trained as a nurse, Val Jordan, who works with her husband, the gynaecologist Joe Jordan, once told me, you understand the exigencies of a workaholic doctor's life, and if you're a fellow barrister, argued Julie MacKenzie, who practised in the same chambers as her husband, Ian Fenny – and even occasionally found herself pitted against him – you can more easily accept the unpredictable hours and missed dinners.

Workaholic political couples such as the Conservative MP and minister Robert Jackson and his wife, Caroline, Conservative MEP for an overlapping constituency, who spends much of her time in Brussels and Strasbourg, enjoy bouncing ideas off each other and sharing expertise. And the film director Christine Edzard lives a euphorically workaholic existence with her husband and producer, Richard Goodwin, in a home which is inextricably intertwined with their company, Sands Films, in Rotherhithe, so that they seldom leave the premises and are 'on duty' twenty-four hours a day – supported by a devoted workaholic staff.

'Colleagues from the same company or profession can fall into an easy shorthand,' says Paula Grayson, 'which does not require the effort of interpretation a stay-at-home partner, or one in a different business, would demand.' And shared work, Dr Martin theorized, encouraged shared emotion.

But what really created a climate in which the female workaholic flourished in the 1980s was divorce – although some would argue that workaholic women were largely to blame for the rising divorce rate!

Nancy Paul, an American psychologist and management consultant who picked up the threads of her career when her marriage broke up, surveyed the careers of 500 divorced or separated men and women from both sides of the Atlantic. Of those polled, as I reported in a feature in *The Times* in 1989, more than half of the women had increased their professional achievement after divorce, with only 25 per cent reporting a decrease, and 47 per cent reported a marked increase in motivation and fulfilment. On the other hand, nearly 42 per cent of the men polled reported a decrease in motivation, achievement and fulfilment – and only 33 per cent an increase. Most significantly Paul found that women often became 'wedded to their work' after their marriages failed, whereas men simply floundered about a bit before 're-investing [their energies] in another relationship with a high probability of failure'. Women workaholics are well aware that they are less likely to enjoy the 'second chance' of a second family than their male counterparts. And the ex-wives of workaholics are frequently infuriated by the way their former husbands dandle and drool over the babies of their dotage (and the bimbos who bear them), when they never had time for the offspring of their early, *striving* years.

The divorced women's urge to throw themselves into their work was not simply in order to support themselves and, sometimes, their children, Paul believed. 'There is more than a bit of competitiveness about it: they want to prove to their ex-husbands that they can do it. It also answers the existential question of "Who am I?".'

Martha Fellowes, an American architect based in Britain, decided to start her own business shortly before her marriage broke up. She had just completed an architecture degree. Paul found that it was quite common for women to 'subconsciously prepare for separation and divorce in this way'. Or, conversely, 'The fact that the woman suddenly wants to achieve more can be a catalyst in the marriage break-up.'

Fellowes – whose daughter was ten at the time the report came out – admitted to me that one of the reasons she worked twelve hours a day was that 'the work does become a substitute for marriage: it's easier to work until seven o'clock at night in the office, where you're in control of things, than to come home at five o'clock to the reality of being a single parent!'

Other women I interviewed on the subject for *The Times* were equally candid. Jackie Houlder, an estate agent who had been divorced for five years when I spoke to her and also had one daughter, said, 'My husband always expected me to be there after school and wouldn't have approved of me working full-time. I could never have done the long hours I am putting in now. I've become more assertive, more my own person.'

Paul's study showed that even divorced women who subsequently found a 'significant other', as Americans coyly call them, are determined to hang on to their careers as a symbol of their hard-won independence so that they will never again find themselves as defenceless as they felt after their divorce. 'They say, "Not on your life – I'll never be dependent again."'

Forty-three-year-old Janette Eames, another woman I spoke to when the report came out, had worked at up to three jobs a week, she said, to support her husband while he trained as a chartered accountant. 'We lived on £4 a week. Then he qualified the minute we got divorced and began making money!' she said somewhat bitterly. She had always dreamed, she told me, of starting her own business and after her divorce, when she was working as a medical laboratory scientist, founded Scientific Staff Consultants, which was, at the time of writing, the biggest business of its kind in the country. 'I can remember making my first £10,000 and phoning my ex-husband to tell him,' she recalled. 'I'm sure I did it partly to prove myself to him, but my prime motivation was deeper. I had to prove myself to me.' After the business was well established she married again – and was in the throes of another separation when we spoke. 'Successful women are often extremely gullible in relationships,' she theorized, 'and are driven to be successful because of the failures in our personal lives.' That said, she added that she would always hire a divorced woman over a married one, all other things being equal, because of 'their tremendous motivation to prove themselves'.

Dr Sheila Rossan, a psychology lecturer at Brunel University and a spokesperson for the Psychology of Women section of the British Psychological Society, told me at the time that she also believed that 'Many successful businesswomen are working hard to compensate for their failed personal lives.' She suggested that how we perceived certain activities as children would determine whether we turned to the bottle, the biscuit tin or the business for solace.

These women may not have been born workaholics. They may not even have intended to work. But just as circumstances turned the fictional heroine Scarlett O'Hara – petted and pampered symbol of the Southern American life of leisure in ante-bellum days – into the obsessive workaholic of the Reconstruction era who couldn't stop finding 'unladylike' ways of making money, even when her husband(s) told her she had more than enough, so the meekest homely type may discover, when her mettle is tested, that there's a tiger – or rather a tycoon – in her tank.

For a wonderfully amusing collection of articles and advertisements from *Good Housekeeping* in the 1920s and 1930s, published in 1991 as *Things My Mother Should Have Told Me* (Ebury Press), the magazine's current editor, Noëlle Walsh, chose a particularly revealing selection on 'Financial Independence for Wives', which was written by Mary Borden in the

1930s. During the First World War, Borden wrote, women:

> gave up doing needlework, got out of the habit of sitting at home, with their children, took to driving motor lorries, running canteens, nursing in hospitals, or packed the children off to school and took the places of their absent men in shops and factories. And they liked it. Of course the women liked it. Many of them were tasting for the first time the freedom of movement men have always had. It was glorious. Wives, mothers, daughters went out each morning into the great, bustling, exciting world to earn their living; and at the end of the week they put their own wages or salaries in their own pockets and felt a glow of satisfaction they had never known before.
>
> Home, husband, children, all looked different, because they saw themselves differently in relation to each. They had discovered that their homes didn't fall to pieces because they left them at nine o'clock every morning. They had found out that their children didn't languish, but on the contrary flourished exceedingly, on a less concentrated diet of mother love; and it had occurred to them that it was humiliating to be obliged to ask a husband for pocket money . . .

This article seems curiously applicable to working women today, many of whom admit that even if there's no change left after paying for the childcare and the train fare, they go to work for the enjoyment, the stimulation, the companionship and the independence it can offer. And possibly because women aren't

automatically expected to work for a living, they are
more likely to work for pleasure.

The Mintel 'Special Report on British Lifestyles' for
1991 made the point that although 'financial necessity
is given as the main reason for working by 62 per cent
of working women . . . 67 per cent would continue to
work even if the money was not needed.' Women,
perhaps, like the Lancashire greengrocer Margaret
Hoare, who 'in accordance with her last wish', the
Daily Telegraph reported, 'was laid out on the vegetable
counter of her shop' because, as a close friend said, she
loved her shop so much!

It would not have surprised Mary Borden that one
of the reasons many women 'take off' at work only
after divorce, as Paul discovered, was that they are no
longer putting in that tiring 'second shift' of supporting
their husbands. 'And that's part of the reason men do
less well after divorce, because they lose that support
system of a hot meal, a warm bed and a clean shirt. For
women the marital home is often just a round of
drudgery which they could do better without.'

The workaholic MP Edwina Currie told men what
they could do if they wanted to come home to a hot
meal and a warm bed: if they wanted the heat, the gist
was, they should be prepared to stand in the kitchen!
Mrs Currie is a woman who harbours no guilt about
her career commitment – or, if she does, she is very
good at camouflaging it. As she writes in her book
What Women Want (Sidgwick & Jackson, 1990):

> I stopped feeling guilty years ago, after one
> weekend when I had been persuaded to go as a
> keen young councillor to a high-powered political
> conference on the future of welfare. My conscience

aching, I slaved for a week putting meals into the fridge and freezer, carefully wrapped and colour-coded, with precise instructions on which to cook for a string of nutritious and wholesome dinners. When I came back, duly fired with political enthusiasm, I found the sink full of dirty plates, the waste bin overflowing with newspaper and the fridge still crammed to bursting with my offerings. Susie, aged nearly three, was summoned. 'Did you manage all right when I was away?' 'Oh, yes, Mummy, it was lovely,' the mite answered with a disarming smile. 'We had fish and chips and 'mato ketchup four times! When are you going away again?'

Other working women – even great and famous ones – have not yet reached Edwina Currie's enviable state of equanimity. Dame Gwyneth Jones, one of the most celebrated dramatic sopranos in the world, told *You* magazine this year, 'I'll stand there in the kitchen cooking and baking for hours, filling up the freezer with nice things so that my husband and daughter will have plenty to eat while I'm away. I practise my scales at the same time because I hate wasting time,' added the diva, who takes her music everywhere with her – even into the bath!

Guilt is usually a constant companion of the working woman, be she tycoon or tea-lady, whether she's a wife and mother or just made to feel guilty about being unnaturally wedded to her career. In 1991 the 'Mummy Doll' – which made her successful début in America as the 'Mommy Doll' in 1990 – was introduced in Britain. The doll, which comes with business suit, briefcase and baby, makes the ideal guilt-edged gift for working mothers to placate their children with, and has been used in playgroups in America to help children come to terms with why their mothers work.

Lucy Daniels, director of the Working Mothers Association in Britain, told *The Times* in 1990, 'Our feeling is that women have been extraordinarily flexible about the problems of combining motherhood with their own and their husband's sense of needing to work. But if they bend any further they will snap.'

Her organization held a conference at the London Business School to respond to figures released from labour force surveys of each member country of the European Community: these showed that one British father in three worked more than fifty hours a week, and 46,000 with children aged eight or under were clocking up an astounding ninety-eight hours – making British *fathers* 'the workaholics of Europe'. So where did that leave British *mothers*? Holding the baby, and holding back their own ambitions.

Yet everywhere, as the 1980s drew to a close, we were hearing that women were being encouraged back into the workforce and would be needed more than ever thanks to the demographic changes which would make women the only ones to 'man' jobs there would not be enough school-leavers to fill. Women were wooed by highly publicized initiatives, such as 'Back to the Future,' a drive to boost the number of women returning to work, sponsored by the Department of Employment and the BBC's *Woman's Hour* in 1990. However, they encouraged a different and discouraging reality.

Women returners told me for articles I did on the subject for *The Times* and *Good Housekeeping* that their experiences with employment agencies and employers had been totally at odds with what they had been primed to expect.

British women were confused on many levels at the dawn of the 1990s – even before the recession and the Gulf War plunged the rest of the world into almost equal uncertainty. Shirley Conran had disowned 'Superwoman', who, she felt, had turned into a bit of a Frankenstein's monster. But was Superwoman really dead, and if so, what aspirational role model had replaced her? Books and articles celebrated the return of the feminine, *womanly* woman, worlds away from the stereotypical workaholic, and while *Working Woman* magazine had failed, numerous new knitwear and sewing pattern purveyors flourished.

She, one of the working woman's oldest friends, metamorphosed into a mother-and-baby magazine, as its editor, Linda Kelsey, former editor of *Cosmopolitan* went, like many of her contemporaries, from being a totally career-oriented 'Cosmo Girl' to a maternal 'new woman' (although she would avoid that expression, because it's the name of a rival magazine).

Whereas in the 1980s there was tremendous pressure to be back at the desk in a miniskirt looking as good and being as efficient as Anna Wintour two weeks after the birth of a baby, a new kind of pressure was growing on women to look for alternative ways to 'have it all' without forswearing their femininity on being required to ape men in order to equal them. 'The human resources director of a large multinational company told me they were having difficulty attracting women into top management posts because the role models there already were women behaving like men, and the younger women didn't want to try to be like

men,' says Christine McNulty of Applied Futures.
'They wanted to work out new ways to be themselves
and still be fulfilled by their work.' Accepting that men
and women might work *differently* and still work out
was undoubtedly a step in the right direction.

Distinctions were drawn between 'masculine' and
'feminine' management styles; feminine curves were
celebrated once again and the baby became the
'designer accessory' featured in advertisements and
fashion shots and all the best places. Now that men
were wearing them (occasionally, at weekends) as a
badge of caring masculinity, it became easier for
women to acknowledge their maternal yearnings.
Fashion firms geared their designs for the new forty-
something *femme fatale* 'with more money and time
on her hands than ever before', as one Eastex press
release put it – although there was considerable
debate about how she would look and, more
importantly, how she would see herself. (The Royal
Society of Arts set a bursary brief for fashion students
to design for her and they came up with everything
from Courrèges-style white plastic mini-dresses to
hobble-skirted Suffragette suits!)

In the late 1980s *Good Housekeeping* began offering a
prize – as a reaction against all those 'Businesswomen
of the Year' and 'Women Mean Business' awards that
had become so fashionable during the decade. Called
'Enterprising Woman' and sponsored by the National
Westminster Bank, it was meant to be for the woman
who had achieved the best balance between family and
working life, which often involved running a business
from home. Women such as thirty-year-old Rosie
Winston, who ran her own successful interior design
business, with the help of her husband, while

mothering two-year-old twins. 'I think because I'm a fulfilled person it makes me a better mother,' she said. 'I think of the company as my eldest child.'

These women may have talked about balancing their lives, but the odds are they were up to all hours balancing the books. And without the professional peers and props that sustained their pioneering sisters, who stormed the nation's boardrooms in their pussycat bows, the new generation of home – or small-business-based workaholics may feel increasingly isolated and confused.

The new emphasis – supposedly – on 'human' values, children and 'home-making' in the 1990s, coupled with the technological developments outlined already in Chapter 4, should conspire to make 'tele-working' an increasingly tempting option for women torn between the two worlds of work and home. But when a woman comes home from the office with her 'power' suit and bulging briefcase, it is arguably more difficult to expect her to begin Dr Arlie Hochschild's 'second shift' than it would be if she was doing the first at home.

Dr Hochschild, a university professor, discovered that women worked roughly fifteen hours longer each week than men, or an extra year of twenty-four-hour days in every twelve-year period. Not surprisingly the studies she consulted showed that 'working mothers were more likely than any other group to be "anxious"', but she also noted that 'working mothers have higher self-esteem and get less depressed than housewives', even if they're said to be tired and sick more often than their working husbands. (Of course, some of those 'sickness' statistics could really be an excuse for childcare commitments which the working mothers were ashamed to admit to and which their husbands didn't share!)

Curiously, despite their double burden, Professor Cooper notices: 'Women seem to cope much better with workplace stress than their male counterparts, possibly because men feel so totally defined by their work and women are better able to balance it against outside interests.' Women workaholics, however, like Margaret Thatcher, define themselves by their work much more than other women – and are often, like Thatcher, in 'mould-breaking' jobs, which, Cooper found, could lead to greater stresses. He cited the female barrister in an all-male chambers as an example.

Margaret Bennett, a solicitor who was the only woman partner in a firm of City solicitors, and has since set up her own law firm, told me for an article on what the Americans call 'the mommy-track' that I wrote for *The Times* back in 1988: 'The big firms with more than 100 partners may have only three or four women – and there are subtle ways in which male partners can affect a woman's morale so that she says it's too much to handle and backs down.'

Bennett, whose two children were five and thirteen at the time, said, 'The moment one becomes pregnant the attitude is, "From now on she is a write-off", and one's equals believe you are not competition any more.' How did she manage to avoid being 'mommy-tracked' – shunted off the 'fast-track'? 'You have to say, "I am going to put my career first and home life second,"' Bennett said without hesitation or guilt. The eight-year gap between her children was deliberate, she explained, because she felt she could not cope with two young children and stay on the 'fast track', and she was back at work two weeks after the birth of her second child. And if she thought she worked hard *then*, Bennett says, it was nothing compared to how hard she's been working since starting her own company!

The need for such strategies and stoic shows of determination put women work enthusiasts under considerable pressure in the 1980s. The film *Baby Boom*, which starred Diane Keaton as a fast-tracker suddenly shunted on to the mommy-track when she 'inherits' a baby from a dead relative, points the way to an even harder ethos for the 1990s. The woman work enthusiast must work out a new way to 'have it all' without sacrificing 'human' values – ideally, the message is, by doing what Keaton does, and starting up a cottage industry selling home-made baby food – or some other palatable product.

In the 1980s the working woman became a style statement. Advertisements were pitched at the same sort of sexy, shoulder-padded women who peopled them. While magazines such as *Working Woman*, which did well in America, failed to work in Britain, this aspirational image of the working woman was flirted with by more frivolous manifestations of the media until even women without the remotest interest in work were eager to emulate her. (Why the 'Mayflower Madam', Sydney Biddle Barrows's call girls, all carried briefcases and were taught how to look like working women, not working girls!)

The caricatured workaholic is inevitably male and the workaholic culture of the 1980s was frequently referred to as 'macho', yet it demanded a masochistic streak, which women are supposed to have in abundance. And a woman accustomed to doing ten things at once at home will be even more likely than a man to take on too many responsibilities at work – particularly if she feels the need to prove herself in that arena. She is ripe for exploitation and a cruel corporate culture of the type described in Anne Wilson Schaef's *The Addictive Organization* (Harper & Row, 1988) may well capitalize on her weakness.

Workaholic women (unless they're also shopaholics, which is quite possible, according to an American psychologist who specializes in treating them both) don't usually pay as much attention to the trappings of the job as to the work in hand. Corner offices and hot-and-cold-running secretaries aren't generally as important to them as to their male counterparts and their reluctance to delegate (possibly *because* they are conditioned to believe they *have* to cope) can burn them out, as Dr Malcolm Carruthers discovered was likely to happen, before their time.

Women told me how because they were aware they lived far away, had to leave early to collect children or had been permitted the 'luxury' of flexitime or job-share options, they felt they had to work that much harder. Two guilty women grateful for the opportunity to job-share are probably the best bet any boss could wish for, because each will give her half a job and half a salary 100 per cent effort.

The caricaturist's image of the female workaholic would probably still be a formidable besuited, bespectacled spinster who had given her life to the firm and looked it – and never let you forget it. But she could be any woman around you – even your secretary, scheming to take your job – as the film *Working Girl* demonstrated. She could be married or divorced, single or a mother returning after what is now known as a 'career break' but used to be called raising children.

The best types – like the (at the time of writing) Black Country Development Corporation and British Nuclear Fuels director Jean Denton, the advertising agency chief Jennifer Laing of Laing, Henry, Hill Holliday and the Barbican director Detta O'Cathain – know how to delegate, 'network' and work as part of a team. Denton is particularly involved in encouraging the women's networking she feels is so important, and in 'mentoring' other women.

The worst (who shall remain nameless) find it terribly difficult to delegate and insist on dictating every letter and chairing every meeting themselves. And they are the ones, particularly if they also derive most of their social life and status from the job, who are in the most danger from their addiction and are most difficult to work with.

Joanna Foster, the workaholic chair of the Equal Opportunities Commission, who lives midway between its two offices in London and Manchester and divides her time between them, believes that there is now an 'ambivalence being experienced by both men and women' in the workplace, and warns, in an essay in *What Women Want*: 'We don't seem to be ready to give up or delegate some of our traditional role as managers on the home front, yet we take on more and more outside and then wonder why we get exhausted.'

Although many women work enthusiasts attempt to channel the same enthusiasm into ironing their husbands' shirts and cleaning the kitchen floor, it can be difficult when they have had a taste of higher forms of fulfilment. Professor Cooper says: 'Once women go out and begin to get kudos and a tangible sense of achievement, it raises their self-esteem.'

When he was only six my son once startled me as I asked him to help me do something in the kitchen by voicing a sentiment his father's lofty attitude to household tasks often implied: 'I can't. I'm having *ideas.*' The inference was that women didn't have ideas – or that, if they did, they shouldn't have them above their station, and should be able to carry on doing the cooking and the washing-up at the same time. Thus many women are accused of being workaholics when they are simply trying to put in what for a man would be considered a normal working week. But because this means they are not always free to collect the children, take the cat to the vet, tax the car, wait in for the electricity-meter reader and pick up their husbands' suits from the drycleaner, they are disparaged as being workaholics with no time for the important things in life, and pressurized – subtly or overtly – until they crack or turn into unwilling 'Superwomen'.

Even the sort of executive women who can afford to hire nannies for their children and household help to ensure that their homes are spotless, errands are done and meals are served on time, can be made to feel guilty about the degree of mental investment they put into their jobs. Their partners – like Jennifer d'Abo's – may require pampering on a grander scale, and hint that if their existing wives won't provide it, they can easily enough find a sweet young thing who will.

At professional functions spouses are expected to attend it is often difficult to tell the married female executives from those who are divorced since both, as one commiserated with me, were likely to turn up on their own. 'I accompany my husband to all his company dinners,' she sighed, 'but he has never come to one of mine.'

So most women work enthusiasts secretly yearn for a 'wife' who will support them in the way workaholic husbands have come to expect to be supported. No one yet runs courses for corporate husbands, the way they do for corporate wives, but Wendy Walden, who specializes in such coaching, has been approached by a few men for advice, she swears.

Denis Thatcher was considered by many to be the ideal example of what the spouse of a female workaholic should be like – so much so that a 'Denis Thatcher Society' (composed of men of considerable power in Washington, DC, whose wives happened to hold high-profile positions in the capital), had sprung up in America to celebrate him. When I visited them, they were tongue-in-cheek about the concept but seriously aware that they were pioneers in uncharted territory.

Henry Kissinger apparently once said that power was the ultimate aphrodisiac. But whereas that is undoubtedly true as far as men are concerned – the ageing autocrat and his bimbos being one of life's great clichés – with women, alas, this is not the case. According to Professor Cooper's study of male and female executives, the sex lives of the women was either unsatisfactory or virtually non-existent, and it was once my happy task, for *The Times*, to contact well-known women of power and ask them how their sex lives were (I'm surprised more of them didn't send me packing!).

Jennifer d'Abo, who, as ex-wife of the tycoon Peter Cadbury, had viewed the 'sex and success' syndrome from both sides, summed it up succinctly. 'A powerful man is attractive – a powerful woman frightening.'

The power of women's passion for their work is particularly frightening to men, who feel neglected or belittled because of it. Until deep-rooted attitudes and expectations alter, even better childcare provision and more enlightened employment policies will not help to save the workaholic woman's marriage, and the cold economic chill of the recession may threaten her hard-won victories in the workplace.

Will the gathering stormclouds darken the rosy dawn of the brave new world demographic change was supposed to create for her? Christine McNulty, who says she never *did* believe that the 1990s would be the 'decade of women', is not worried. She considers the recession 'a temporary blip' in the grand scheme of things, and thinks we will see more women simply deciding, of their own free, inner-directed will, to choose *between* career and family rather than greedily attempting to 'have it all'. 'In the leading-edge groups women are saying, "Either I'll have a career and not have children or have children and not have a career", and that will filter down to other groups as the decade progresses,' she prophesies.

Be that as it may, the choice is no longer so clear-cut – nor it is clear any longer why only women have to make it.

One interesting development on the horizon should free the female workaholic of some of the additional pressures that her male counterpart does not have to bear. The ability to freeze ova – not just sperm or fertilized embryos – could be the breakthrough dedicated career women have long dreamed of. Theoretically it means that eggs can be removed from a woman at her most fertile period in her early twenties, and stored until she is ready to have them fertilized by the sperm of her choice – at a time she feels *really* ready to take a career break.

What a boon this will be to women doctors, lawyers and others in fast-paced, hierarchical professions where to miss out a few years before your mid-thirties means to be left behind!

As I reported in *The Times* in 1990, even post-menopausal wombs can now be 'prepped' for pregnancy, and once the egg-freezing technique is perfected and popularized, it will mean the female workaholic will be able to ignore the ticking of her biological clock as well as the real one.

7

All Work and No Play?

'The dynamic principle of fantasy is play, which belongs also to the child, and as such it appears to be inconsistent with the principle of serious work. But without this playing with fantasy no creative work has ever yet come to birth.'

Carl Jung

'No man is really happy or safe without a hobby and it makes precious little difference what the outside interest may be – botany, beetles or butterflies . . . anything will do so long as he straddles a hobby and rides it hard.'

Sir William Osler

'Wholeness' is something workaholics are often accused of lacking, and in this supposedly holistic age it is no longer admirable to be doggedly two-dimensional. 'Workafrolics' such as Richard Branson, who combine a workaholic dedication to their business with passions for more frolicsome pastimes (in Branson's case, hot-air ballooning), are more in tune with the mood of the 'New Age'.

But it is possible to be as 'driven' about hobbies as about work, so that for some people even relaxation becomes a competitive event – and places an additional strain on families and friendships. As the leading divorce lawyer Peter Grose-Hodge noted, it is not so much work as the way leisure hours are allocated that becomes the last straw which leads to divorce – and the short, sharp squash game engaged in by two highly competitive Type As is not just a dubiously beneficial but a dangerous recreation.

There are nearly as many paths to 'wholeness' as to nirvana – and to the confirmed workaholic both may seem equally apocryphal. Work enthusiasts find it easier to work at the work they enjoy, rather than working towards achieving the kind of 'balance' which is currently deemed to be desirable yet can enforce its own tyranny.

If your work is also your hobby and your relaxation, it is usually not the sort of work that would count as putting all your eggs in one basket. And you may well be happier and more fun to live with than someone who had a nine-to-five attitude to a routine job and then obsessively builds castles out of matchsticks or puts ships in bottles in his or her spare time.

The prolific behavioural scientist and management consultant Professor Charles Handy, a leading proponent of what he calls 'portfolio living', keeps a fresh perspective through his habit of filing different types of work in different, figurative, 'portfolios' and taking them out when it suits him. He told me that he goes to his country home to write – a book a year; while in London Professor Handy (at the time of writing, Visiting Professor at the London Business School and Vice-President of the Royal Society of Arts) has a much more frenetically workaholic life of lectures, meetings and speeches. In the country he cooks – 'competitively', says his wife, Elizabeth, a photographer who shares (and often illustrates) his portfolio existence. He says he took up cooking 'because it uses another part of the brain. I write for five hours each morning, until 1.30 pm, when I'm in the country, and you need an antidote.'

Most healthy and successful work enthusiasts like the Handys have already – subconsciously or not – worked out their own 'coping strategies' which weave elements of enjoyment and relaxation into their work and daily lives.

Dame Shirley Porter, who this year resigned as leader of Westminster Council – some speculated to become Lord Mayor – told *Cosmopolitan*, 'I either go for a relaxing massage or aromatherapy or belt a ball around a tennis court' when she is not being driven on by what the *Daily Telegraph* called 'an atavistic pleasure in "getting things done".' Joanna Foster, chair of the Equal Opportunities Commission, says that 'Building in "me" time is important. Sundays are sacrosanct for spending with my family or friends.' RCA Records' UK Managing Director Lisa Anderson says, 'My assistant is always a good monitor of my state of stress. When it reaches a certain point she delivers a large glass of wine to my desk. That usually does the trick. (Always after 6 pm, though, and only about four times a year!)' Tracy Edwards, MBE, skipper of the Whitbread Round-the-World Race winner *Maiden* admitted, 'I work best under stress but when it reaches a certain level I just like to be at home, alone, to mull things over', and the MP Emma Nicholson says, 'My stress point is when there's no stress. I thrive on it and challenge myself to create it.'

For me the constant variety of my work brings its own refreshment. One day I may be trundling through the countryside to interview some reclusive celebrity, the next rushing to report on a major conference about employment issues, the third, perhaps, on a photographic shoot for a magazine article on stately homes, the fourth on the telephone setting up a series on complementary medicine and the fifth producing a shopping column and researching a feature on workaholics.

Weekends are for catching up on work-related reading and writing longer, more contemplative articles which do not have an overnight deadline (in addition, of course, to the normal weekend activities of shopping, cooking, ferrying the children to ballet and computer classes, having their friends round, having *our* friends round and collapsing in front of the television with a good bottle of wine).

But then, as a self-employed person, I can organize my schedule so that I can occasionally pick up my children from school and enjoy midweek activities with them, which would be out of the question for mothers who work nine to five but keep their weekends strictly free.

I find that regular swimming and jogging help to put the work into perspective, and that if I go for periods without them because I'm rushing for too many early-morning trains or (as when writing this book) crouched in front of a word-processor for too long, I begin to feel (and look) distinctly ratty.

I was amused to learn from the great American exercise guru Callan Pinckney – the woman reputed to have pared down the Duchess of York's pear-shaped figure – when I interviewed her for the *Sunday Times Magazine*, that when she was writing one of her best-selling exercise books she concentrated to such a degree that she couldn't find the time to exercise and found her famous taut bottom getting 'gooshy' – her word for flabby. 'Superwoman' Shirley Conran once confessed to me that when she was in the final throes of a best-selling novel she would let her normally well-disciplined figure and almost everything else go to pot, knowing she could easily deal with any excesses in the euphoric afterglow of achievement – a personal exercise trainer, another growth industry of the 1980s, calls daily at her Monte Carlo home – and she regularly swims in the sea.

Anne Wilson Schaef suggests that work addicts sometimes resort to props, which she sees as subsidiary addictions, such as exercise, food, cigarettes or caffeine. To her those who boast that they work hard and play hard may be doubly addicted – and, indeed, exercise addiction was one of many newly diagnosed afflictions of the 1980s.

But then, all project-based work enthusiasts (authors, actors, athletes, solicitors, account executives, etc.) have periods of peak effort counterbalanced by slacker times when they can take stock of their lives, ease off on coffee and cigarettes, start exercising again or eat more healthily. If they are well-balanced work enthusiasts, they will.

Such people are worlds away from the dispirited drones who drink, smoke or take drugs to alleviate boredom or to interject a 'kick' into uninspired lives.

It is workers confined to a regular, relentless routine with no respite and a sense of being swept along by circumstances beyond their control who are, experts largely seem to agree, in most danger of reaching a brittle breaking-point.

When does a workaholic need help? When the workaholic knows he or she needs it. *You* know who you are out there, and you don't really need any book (or well-meaning busybody) to tell you when it's time to try to stop, or at least slow down, the whirl.

The actor Timothy Dalton described the feeling well in an interview in the *Daily Mail* in 1990. The James Bond star said, 'I have worked too much over the past five years. Many times I've finished one job on a Saturday and started the next on the Monday. It's had a bad effect on my personal life. I don't seem to have a non-work life at all any more. I sometimes wonder who I am. When you are sleeping four or five hours a night and putting all your energy into your latest project, you begin to lose a bit of yourself.'

Perhaps you first knew when you bent to perfunctorily kiss your children goodbye and their heads were so much higher than you remembered. Or maybe it's the way your wife has stopped even *attempting* to communicate with you and has been spending so much time with the gamekeeper . . . what was his name, again? Mellors?

Did the penny drop when your children consistently ran for comfort to the au pair, a pair of old socks or any passing stranger – but certainly not to you? Or was it a health scare – like that twinge of angina every time there was a big deal to clinch or the way your heart began wildly palpitating as you lay in bed reviewing the day's work and ruminating on the next?

Whatever it was, you know that what once seemed like a magic roundabout has become a tedious treadmill and you want to get off. Instead of that heady sense of challenge and achievement, you have begun to feel as if your work is controlling you – even (oh horrible, most horrible!) as if you are merely working, like lesser mortals, to pay the mortgage.

Fortunately it is the compulsive workaholic who has never actually *enjoyed* his or her work, or the enforced and unwilling workaholic caught up (for what Christine NcNulty would consider 'sustenance-driven' or 'outer-directed' motives) in a corporate culture which demands a crushing conformity, who is more likely to become such a casualty – not the inner-directed work enthusiast.

For the former, some serious psychotherapy may be the only appropriate answer, to determine whether work is an avoidance activity which masks a deeper, unacknowledged need. The latter, meanwhile – and the organizations they work for – may benefit from the corporate counselling and other progressive moves a company can make, which will be discussed in

Chapter 8. But work enthusiasts who have become a bit too enthusiastic about their work and have, in the process, lost enthusiasm for other things, been ignoring their family and letting friendships slide, may benefit from some of the supposedly life-enhancing and stress-relieving activities and techniques which have become one of the great boom businesses of the past decade.

An increasingly insistent and competitive industry has sprung up to promote displacement activities for people who may or may not be using work as a displacement activity in the first place. Those who can't be bothered to work out their own personally tailored relaxation 'strategy' can choose from hundreds of off-the-peg (and off-the-wall) solutions, from 'mind spas' – an American import involving eye-masks and lots of flashing lights – to health spas. Their proponents promise they can turn the most jaded workaholic into that most desirable of the species, the 'workafrolic' – or at least help him or her to recover the spring in their step and that wonderful feeling of jumping joyously out of bed with childlike excitement at the prospect of the day, instead of lying there groaning like the average work-ambivalent.

I once criticized my son for getting up at the crack of dawn and heading straight to his computer instead of tidying up his room, making himself a nourishing breakfast and getting properly dressed. 'Why shouldn't I? You do the same,' he shot back. Luckily I laughed – for the surest sign that someone is under stress (psychologists specializing in the sort of 'stress management' seminars that have become so popular in Britain over the last few years seem to concur) is the loss of a sense of humour. If you never had one in the first place, don't worry. But if you've got to the stage where you're no fun any more – for yourself or for others – there's little point in (figuratively) laughing all the way to the bank.

Carl Jung said that no creative work was ever accomplished without some playing with fantasy – and it is that playful sense that the worn-out, or burnt-out, workaholic lacks.

Crispin Tweddell, chairman of the forward-thinking British retail consultancy the Piper Trust, is a champion of what he calls 'brain fitness' and believes that mind games are as important as physical exercise for desk-bound executives. 'You can jog in the brain,' he told me for a feature I did on 'Exercising the mind' in *The Times* in 1989.

Tweddell exercised his mind and came up with the idea of marketing a brain-fitness workout for busy executives. In early 1991 it is still in the early warm-up phase, but the Piper Trust has introduced many innovative ideas aimed at reducing stress among its enthusiastic and highly motivated staff and some of the major retail chains it advises.

Tweddell believes that executives can be too 'busy' to be creative, and always reminds those he counsels, 'It's every executive's responsibility to be imaginative as well as to be executive. To think the unthinkable.' To do so they must develop the sense of mental playfulness which will, Tweddell contends, keep their minds flexible enough to prevent them from falling into a workaholic rut. True work enthusiasts – who are often 'Renaissance' people interested and involved in many projects at the same time – probably do this instinctively. Others may need help.

Initially Tweddell recommends 'Herrmann Brain

Dominance' testing to determine what sector of each employee's brain is dominant, so that balanced teams can be built and areas of weakness worked upon. 'We counsel people in that,' says Tweddell. 'If the brain is exercised down only one line, its creativity will dry up.'

So a financial whizz might be set mind-expanding tasks such as painting or going on nature walks, while an airy-fairy creative type would be disciplined with exercises in mathematical precision. 'Love a pine cone,' Herrmann advises the former, while the latter should find balancing their bank statements more beneficial. The Ned Herrmann system has been used for some time in America, where Herrmann is said to have designed and led workshops on creativity for companies such as Shell, IBM, DuPont and AT&T. There is currently a Herrmann Institute in Britain, in Cranbrook, Kent.

IBM is among those companies which has launched a 'creative and innovative thinking programme' involving brainstorming sessions and brain exercises. 'We'll do things like place a pile of rubbish in the centre of a room and each person has to pick something and then discourse for a few minutes on "why life is like a . . . spanner",' an IBM spokeswoman told me for my 'Exercising the mind' feature in *The Times*. 'We think it carries back to their work. It changes attitudes and encourages positivity.'

Dr David Weeks, with whom I collaborated in 1990 on a series for the *Sunday Times Magazine* on 'Brain Fitness', also advocates brain exercises, although he disputes much of Herrmann's theory and practice. Dr Weeks's brain exercises for minimizing the effects of dementia are in use in hundreds of clinics in Britain and around the world. He believes that similar processes can stimulate healthy brains. 'Brains need challenge and interaction,' Dr Weeks told me. 'A weekly routine of brain exercises should be integrated into the working environment – but there is little point in executives doing them if they continue to smoke heavily and go out for boozy lunches. That kills more brain cells than brain exercises bring back!'

For a while the Piper Trust held communal drawing sessions – involving 'copying a picture upside-down to get rid of inhibitions about not being able to draw'. But Tweddell confesses, in retrospect, that 'they didn't work. We had everyone sit around the table once a fortnight and try drawing and it was a kind of *agony*! Too much groupism can become as much an inhibitor as a refreshment. Information is serendipitous and comes out of *encounter*. You need to meet people, see things and hear them, and a balanced diet of inputs is as important as a balanced diet in the office canteen. 'In ecological thinking,' as he puts it for the 1990s, 'everything must be held in proper balance.'

So now each employee is encouraged to work out his or her own personal balancing act. For Tweddell it involves music therapy (he became a trustee of the Marylebone Music Therapy Unit), and he finds that for him playing the piano is a great reliever of the pressures of his demanding and absorbing job. 'I don't learn music by note and rote,' he told me for a feature I did in 1990 on unusual stress relief techniques for the *Sunday Express Magazine*. 'I want it to be a relaxation, not another piece of neurosis in my life.' Organizations such as the Marylebone Music Therapy Unit and individual music therapists are increasingly tuning into the needs of strung-out businesspeople as well as autistic children. Margaret Lobo, a music therapist who worked through the centre, told me how many of her pupils had been referred to her by doctors because of stress, and how she combined vocal lessons with meditation and breathing exercises to help 'the whole person'.

It was Mrs Thatcher's lack of hobbies and interests outside the job which caused experts to voice concern for her health when she was no longer Prime Minister. While she was asking for whom the bell tolled, her successor's wife, Norma Major, was busily bell-ringing – a hobby she enthused was 'one of the most relaxing pastimes' because 'it's very difficult to learn and it gives you a very satisfying feeling to have power over such a heavy object. It's both a physical exercise and a mental challenge.'

Admittedly Mrs Major took ten years to write the biography of Joan Sutherland which seems to have been her major life's work, but many bell-ringing groups around the country are composed of highly stressed, highly pressured high-flyers who ring in order to ring some changes in their fast-paced lives.

I discovered this while researching my feature on stress relief methods for the *Sunday Express Magazine*, and all those I interviewed agreed that the 'deep concentration' required for bell-ringing helped them to unwind. One City financial dealer – at his desk from 7.30 am until after 6 pm – had even met his wife, an equally hard-working computer analyst, through bell-ringing and was convinced their shared hobby cemented their relationship.

Juggling is another playful 'wholeness hobby' which is catching on among high-flyers. *She* magazine proudly dedicates itself to its 'juggler' readers (women

who juggle the demands of a job, husband and
children), although that is probably the kind of juggler
Anne Wilson Schaef is talking about in her manual
Meditations for Women Who Do Too Much when she says:
'Jugglers aren't paid very well and sometimes they get
hit on the head with balls they have in the air.' The
kind of juggling taught by Max and Susi Oddball
appeals to highly paid, hard-headed high-achievers
accustomed to keeping their eyes on the ball.

When I turned up for one of their classes in London
an opera singer, a motorcycle courier and a City
financier were among a mixed bag of fellow pupils – all
of whom (however high or lowly, workaholic or work-
ambivalent) insisted they were suffering from occupational stress.

Max now takes his act out to banks (you've heard of
the listening bank; have you heard about the juggling
bank?) and other organizations; he gives lectures in
business management based upon his juggling
experience and the belief that juggling can help people
withstand the stress of success while coming to terms
with the possibility of failure. I went expecting failure
and was amazed to be able to catch anything – and to
come away feeling as I must have done after attending
a fellow three-year-old's birthday party. Susi got
everyone throwing to each other and built up a strong
sense of trust and camaraderie. 'It is relaxing because
the mind is forced to concentrate on the new
experience,' Susi explained. Max jokes: 'Juggling is
easier to carry around with you than a skiing holiday –
and can have the same effect.'

Tony Buzan, a management consultant, author and
founder of a mind-expanding organization he calls the
Brain Club, went further. 'Juggling is the perfect

balancing mechanism for both the body and the brain,' he told me. 'I always keep some balls on my desk and practise four or five times a day. When I'm juggling I have to pay attention. It uses both the left and right cerebral hemispheres and it obliges me to use rhythm, a great relaxant.' Remember, though – workaholics are often accused of keeping too many balls in the air!

Professor Cary Cooper believes that active work enthusiasts often require active ways of relaxing. 'For me something like a flotation tank would be just too boring,' he says.

Lydia Wong and her partner, Anthony Kennedy, cater to those who are seeking an active method of stress relief in their active lives who feel they wouldn't have the patience to lie still. They teach people to 'dance *with* your stress' through what they call qi-netics (pronounced chi-netics) – a combination of tai chi, callisthenics and meditation which they have developed.

Ms Wong, from Singapore, is a Shiatsu masseuse who has literally walked all over such diverse clients as *He-man* actor Dolph Lundgren, *Witches* star Anjelica Huston and the Sheik of Abu Dhabi. A work enthusiast herself, she travels the world with wealthy clients but spreads the gospel of qi-netics at a church in west London for a few pounds a session.

'It's about taking responsibility for your stress on yourself, and learning to play with it rather than being eaten by it or beaten by it,' says Ms Wong. 'With Shiatsu everyone wants you to take their tension away, but the bottom line is you have to do it yourself.'

Her exercises build up what she describes as 'dynamic tension' to act as a physical counterpoint to the 'creative tension' some workers experience because of their own or their organization's workaholic ethic. In at least one newspaper office I know, 'creative tension' is the editor's euphemism for the fear he engenders to keep everyone on their toes!

But many workaholics can find more passive forms of relaxation equally rewarding. Both Dr Desmond Kelly and Dr Malcolm Carruthers practise a form of meditation as a counterpoint to their hectic careers. Dr Kelly recommends it and Dr Carruthers and his wife, Vera Diamond, both teach a Westernized version, called autogenic training, which is aimed at those to whom meditation is too redolent of Eastern mysticism. Like the Oddballs, Dr Carruthers likens his form of relaxation to 'going on holiday – inside yourself' – a more active terminology which appeals to those who don't like to think of emptying their minds.

Jill Woolfenden, workaholic communications manager for a big international advertising conglomerate, was one of Dr Carruthers's success stories. I interviewed her for the *Sunday Express Magazine*. She was thirty-five, single, with no children and told me, 'I could be at my desk twenty-four hours a day. I was getting to the stage where I'd be talking to Australia in the morning and dealing with problems in San Francisco until late at night, and when I did get home I just wasn't able to switch off. I had difficulty relaxing and was experiencing butterflies in my stomach.' After autogenic training she was sleeping much better, and felt more in control of her working life.

Dr Carruthers insists that it would be wrong to attempt to describe autogenic training in detail here, because to attempt it on the basis of what you read would be 'as dangerous as trying to learn to drive a car from a manual'. So don't attempt it. (Courses will set you back by about £200.) But at its simplest it involves controlled breathing 'and a sequence of mental exercises focusing on sensations of heaviness and warmth in the body', Dr Carruthers says. 'The lovely thing about autogenic training is that it can be done at the desk, on a train or in a plane. It has been designed for people on a tight schedule.'

He claims his clients come off tranquillizers 'and even beta-blockers because it can lower both blood pressure and cholesterol levels. It used to be a secret weapon of the East and West German athletic teams, and has been used by the British rowing and skiing teams.'

There are today almost as many confusing 'relaxation' and 'stress relief' strategies as there are diets and exercise programmes, so that the relaxation business looks in danger of becoming as stressfully competitive as any other. Stephen Palmer, director of the Centre for Stress Management in London, expressed his concern to me: 'Relaxation can become a "fix" like anything else, and people can relax competitively while still being quite stressed.'

Dr David Lewis designs his exercises for stressed-out executives in such a cunning way that this is (theoretically, at least!) impossible. He hooks them up to electronic devices which enable them to 'drive' little trains around, powered by their brainwaves. 'The thing is that their minds have to be in a completely relaxed state to produce the correct frequency of brainwave to move the train – so that the more competitive they become about wanting to make their trains move fast, the worse they do,' Dr Lewis chuckles.

Stephen Palmer believes that 'changing how you view your life can be more important than rushing to some supposed relaxation therapy.' Exercises in altering perception can be extremely useful in converting what Dr Lewis defines as harried Type H people – who hurry, are full of hostility, and prone to heart disease – into constructive Type Cs, who treat threats as challenges, and feel in control of their lives. The time-urgent workaholic who fumes futilely in a traffic jam because he or she is going to be late for a meeting could learn to channel that energy and frustration much more profitably into some 'quality thinking', which could make them arrive at the meeting with new ideas. Numerous 'stress management' and 'time management' consultants purport to be able to help people do just this.

Dan Stamp, of Priority Management, makes the point that 'We spend five hours a week simply looking for things on our desk . . . over two hours a week on unnecessary phone calls' and '30 per cent of meetings are non-productive', even though on average business-people spend twenty-one weeks a year at them, while 22 per cent, he discovered, spend less than fifteen minutes a day with their children.

If we were better able to prioritize, the theory is, we would be better able to perceive threats as challenges and less likely to waste what Dr David Lewis calls our 'stress currency' in frustration. And we would know when it was really necessary to slow down and take on less work, or whether we could simply handle our existing work more effectively – and enjoyably. Although pure time management will not be of much help to the workaholic who feels compulsively driven, it may be of enormous value to those who feel swamped simply because they're disorganized. (Keeping a diary of what you've actually accomplished during a week may bring some surprising revelations!)

In America the former priest Earnie Larson preaches that workaholics – like himself – 'need to practise playing'. He teaches that skill in Minneapolis, lecturing, according to *People* magazine, to over 50,000 people a year and selling over $750,000 worth of tapes. 'Start small,' he advises workaholics. 'Don't try to jump off the treadmill all at once. Take ten minutes when you first get home just to talk to your wife. Try taking Friday afternoons off. You'll feel guilty, lazy, worthless. Just tell yourself you're worthwhile whether you're working or not.' According to Larson, the way you can tell whether your pressures come from within rather than from the workplace is 'if you feel nothing you do is ever good enough'.

One of the drawbacks of many of the 'coping strategies' or 'wholeness hobbies' recommended for workaholics is that they are really what my husband (and he should know!) calls 'strategies for selfishness'. He is a pastmaster at countering his own work stress through 'selfishness strategies', such as outings to football and cricket matches, long country walks and other entertainments in which he prefers not to involve his family. Such strategies can be more alienating, as the matrimonial lawyer Peter Grose-Hodge observed, than an excessive workload.

Workaholics who feel confident that their own lives are balanced should make sure they are not balanced on a knife-edge – and that they have taken their families and friendships into the equation as well. For workaholics who involve their families in their work, and share their enthusiasm for it with them, may be

better balanced than those who meticulously divide
their lives into recreation and relaxation times but
have become totally independent of family and friends
in the process.

The general consensus among experts I have
spoken to is that workaholics who sense they are in
trouble should slow down and take stock, maybe write
out what they enjoy about their work – and their
personal lives – and what they would like to change.
They should involve their families in the process, and
prioritization, delegation and relaxation should be
among their major aims. 'Workaholics are notoriously
bad at delegating,' Dr Weeks has found. 'You must
learn your own personal strengths and weaknesses –
and your personnel and their strengths and weaknesses – and learn to delegate accordingly. Set
yourself realistic deadlines only, allowing sufficient
time to *pace* yourself. Learn what your pace is and don't
try to exceed it.

'Practise "brainstorming" techniques to encourage
innovation instead of always having your head down
at "busy" work. Learn how to act on constructive
advice from your family and the colleagues whose
opinions you respect, and modify your life-style
accordingly – while recognizing that most life-style
changes take place only slowly. And practise some
kind of physical and psychological relaxation – both a
muscular relaxation and a mental one – but catch
yourself if you're turning relaxation or leisure
activities into work.'

Dr Weeks – who finds listening to music a great
relaxant (like the government minister David Mellor,
who listens to loud, classical music constantly while
working and is known for bringing his 'ghetto-blaster'

to the office) – cites a Christmas card he once received from a researcher. 'It said, "What is the secret of Santa's good health and happiness? Is it his diet? Is it the amount of fresh air he gets? Is it because he's so good? No – it's because he does nothing for 364 days a year!"'

Finally, one of the most important things a workaholic can learn is how to say 'no' (a word you've probably said all too often to family and friends!). That is particularly difficult if you genuinely enjoy the work you are asked to do. Timothy Dalton summed up the workaholic's dilemma when he told the *Daily Mail*, 'Trouble is, if work is offered and I want to do it, I can't refuse.' And everyone knows that for an actor being out of work is a much greater cause of stress than too much work.

Unlike an alcoholic or cigarette smoker or other types of anti-social addicts, the workaholic cannot (in most cases), and would never want to, completely abandon the substance of his addiction. Working it into a balanced life with plenty of playfulness, love and laughter distinguishes the dynamo from the drone.

Towards a New Balance

'The master word [work] . . . is the open sesame to
every portal, the great equalizer in the world, the true
philosopher's stone, which transmutes all the base
metal of humanity into gold.'

Sir William Osler

When the Employment Secretary Norman Fowler
announced, at the dawn of 1990, that he would be
resigning his cabinet post in order to spend more time
with his family, the move was heralded as symbolic of
the New Age of humanitarian values which, we had
been promised, was just around the corner. Time,
according to the American futurist, Faith Popcorn,
would become the most valuable commodity of the
1990s.

Sir Norman voiced the fears of many men – and
women – caught up in the workaholic whirl of the
1980s when he said, 'Some things you can put on a
shelf. My embryo novel, for instance. But you can't
take the children down from the shelf ten years later.'
Or, as jewellery magnate Gerald Ratner likes to
remind himself, 'Nobody ever wished on their death
bed they'd spent more time in the office.'

When I spoke to Sir Norman a year later (to try to

find out whether the change had really made a difference, or whether, with his workaholic nature, work was *still* expanding to fill time) he said that what had most amazed him were 'the tremendous number of letters of support' he had received for his decision – some from men saying that they wished they had the courage to do the same, and a surprising number from men who said they *had*.

'I got support from some surprising quarters where I wouldn't have expected it,' he chuckled. 'What impressed me were the number of people who felt the same – people you wouldn't necessarily feel would do so. People wanting to be a bit more master of their own destinies and not afraid of getting off the promotion treadmill.'

Fiona Stewart, Associate Director of Social Research at the Henley Centre for Forecasting, told *The Times* on learning of Norman Fowler's resignation, 'Men are starting to define themselves in terms of their family and their interests rather than their jobs. The job is dropping down the list as a source of pride.' Her research showed that 77 per cent considered their family their most important source of pride, 61 per cent health and fitness and only 46 per cent their jobs. But, of course, what people say and what they do are often two entirely different things. My own husband showed me a survey he had filled out about himself for a 'stress management' exercise at work, and I didn't recognize the man I knew at all from the answers!

Sir Norman was putting the finishing touches to his memoirs and was enjoying 'being around' at home more, and becoming acquainted with his two daughters, Kate and Isobel. (Kate's birth, he recalled, had interrupted a Remembrance Day service, Isobel's a

Cabinet meeting.) Although he had accrued three directorships in the interim, he said, he insisted, 'I'm far more master of my own diary than I have been for fifteen years.' His wife, Fiona, had realistic expectations. 'I don't think he's actually going to spend his time looking after the children,' she told journalists at the time. 'But he might be able to turn up to school plays and meetings with teachers.'

Lady Fowler, who made use of the 'job-sharing' option available at the House of Commons library to facilitate combining motherhood with a career, considers her husband a chronic workaholic, and laughed uproariously when she went to 'drag him away from his word processor' to tell me whether he was working less and enjoying it more in the 1990s. But they had been going over proofs of the book *together*, and they both felt that his priorities had changed. In many senses the Fowlers (even though, or possibly because, this is a second marriage for each of them) could be said to typify the sort of family who will help us work out new role models for the 1990s. They haven't 'dropped out' of the rat race in the way the 'good life' drop-outs of the 1960s did; they have simply slowed down enough to have time to look around and appreciate the moment, as well as making sure they're really heading in the direction they want to go. They have tried to work out a blueprint for a more balanced future.

'Balance' is the buzzword for the 1990s. Susan Butenhoff, a British public relations executive who now lives and works in California, says: 'Balance seems to be what everyone's looking for. This year we are launching a product called Perfect Balance – a 'half-caf' coffee, for people who don't obsessively want to cut out all the caffeine but are concerned about having too much.' But in the pursuit of perfect balance we must be careful not to create too bland a blend. Genius and creativity are often *un*balanced, like many of the workaholics who have been imbued with them, although as a corporate psychologist once confided to me, 'Most organizations would prefer to forgo one or two oddball geniuses for a 1 per cent overall improvement.'

Butenhoff – a workaholic work enthusiast who is usually in her office at 7 am, seldom leaves before 10 pm and takes files along in her handbag even when she goes out on a dinner date, 'so I can review them if the other person leaves the table' – says, 'A lot of people in the office got together and created a "get a life" quiz, as we called it. It had multiple-choice questions like, 'At home your plants are (a) healthy, (b) dead, (c) you don't even buy plants because you know you won't have time to look after them; when you're at a party you (a) talk about your job a third of the time, (b) don't talk about your job at all, (c) are totally offended if the whole party doesn't revolve around your job; when you're on vacation you (a) call in when you arrive, check for messages and leave your number, (b) never call in and don't leave a number (c) leave telephone, fax, secondary emergency number *and* call in every day . . . If you answered (c) for everything – as I did – you needed to "get a life" for yourself – and, believe me, a lot of people are talking about that right now in America.'

As *Fortune* magazine reported in 1990 in its feature entitled 'Is your company asking too much?', 'It isn't just the drones at the water cooler who are thinking anew about the burden of hard work, either. It is

senior executives and ambitious yuppies – men and
women who have been running flat out for years –
who have been keeping such thoughts bottled up
inside for fear of appearing weak or uncommitted.'
The article quoted a business professor at Carnegie
Mellon University, Robert Kelley, as saying: 'It used to
be that sixty-hour workweeks gave you warrior
status, but the trend is reversing. People are saying
that sixty-hour weeks mean something is wrong with
the system or the person.'

But according to the poll conducted in conjunction
with the article, 77 per cent of chief executive
organizations believed that, 'US corporations will
have to push their managers harder than ever in order
to compete internationally. Only 9 per cent believe
that restructuring and getting leaner has resulted in
pushing managers *too* hard. If we want to compete
against the Japanese, goes this line of thought, don't
we have to work the same kind of hours they do?'

Time magazine, however, in a recent feature on
sleep deprivation, noted that, 'If any nation can be said
to be suffering greater sleep loss than the US, it may
be Japan. Officeworkers in Tokyo often commute for
an hour or more, arriving at their desks at 9 am and
staying until 8 pm or later. Then they go out to eat and
drink with colleagues, an essential part of the job, and
catch the last train home at midnight. Workers only
get 113 days off a year, compared with Americans' 134
and Germans' 245 . . .' No wonder the Japanese have a
word for killing yourself through overwork!

A psychologist counselling executives on Wall
Street told *Fortune* he thought, 'Developing the proper
balance is such a fine line and requires so much
wisdom I don't know if enough senior managers have

experienced enough trauma in their own personal lives to be that wise.'

This was confirmed in conversations I had with senior executives in Britain, who said they'd *heard* exciting things about the changes around the corner but hadn't yet experienced them. Moira Black, a partner in Price Waterhouse in London and a founder member of the City Women's Network, told me early in 1991 for an article I was writing for *The Times*, 'I agree with the principle that there's more to life than earning a living, and I feel there are changes going on and everybody talks about it, but I'm afraid I'm not seeing much. My hours don't depend on my attitude, they depend on what needs doing . . . Maybe younger people *will* change, but in order for change it is necessary for colleagues to have the same attitudes.' Black, who is married to a civil servant and has no children, says she usually arrives at the office by 8.30 am (when she doesn't have an 8 am breakfast meeting) and seldom leaves before 7.30 pm.

Vivienne Walker, Vice-President of the Institute of Personnel Management at the time of writing and chair of its Organization and Human Resources Planning Committee, told me, 'There are numerous examples of people who work ever harder and achieve increasingly less in a vicious spiral. Yet there is still the expectation that a "company man" is someone who will work sixty hours a week.' And in a recession, when jobs are scarce, the temptation is to run even faster on that treadmill simply to stay in the same place.

Turning vicious spirals – and circles – into virtuous ones, 'driven' workaholics into motivated work enthusiasts, must be a priority, everyone seems to agree, for the 1990s. The only debate is how to go about it. For the moment people are having to work it out for themselves.

Susan Anthony, thirty-seven and single – the archetypal 'corporate woman' of the 1980s – was an analyst in European equities at a big bank in the City of London when I spoke to her early in 1991. She said she sensed the beginnings of a new mood even among the most enthusiastic proponents of the workaholic ethic. She told me, 'Money is still important – I've got a massive mortgage and livery bill to pay – but I obviously want to spend some time with my horse! There was a time when we were always here until 10 at night, and that was crazy. We still work hard – we get in at 7.45 am – but I try to leave at 6.30 now if I can. You could still work every hour of the day, but I don't any more. It could have more to do with the stage I'm at more than anything happening in the company or the country, though.'

This is a very perceptive point. Bob Tyrrell of the Henley Centre for Forecasting points out that the 'Me Generation' of the 1960s (of which he considers himself a representative) has been very much making the running and leading the trends because they do dominate demographically. If they (or should I say we?) are reaching a communal mid-life crisis, a time when people traditionally step back and assess their lives, could that explain the curious and somewhat confused new mood?

The Fowlers had hit what Lady Fowler called 'a natural watershed', when her husband made his momentous decision. She had just turned forty, her husband fifty. 'At times like that you start vaguely thinking what the next ten years will bring,' she told

The Times. 'You reassess your priorities.'

Back in the 1980s Christine McNulty of Applied Futures suggested to me that we would be seeing many more people experiencing a 'change of life' that actually *changed* their lives – turning a period traditionally thought to be a 'crisis' into a dramatic and exciting time.

Liverpool Football Club's manager Kenny Dalglish shocked the sports world when he quit just seven months into a five-year contract worth £1.25 million. He said, 'The biggest problem was the pressure I was putting myself under in my desire to be successful . . . and if the decision had been delayed much longer it certainly wouldn't have been beneficial to me or the club.' Graham Souness also made headlines in 1991 for switching jobs to be near to his children. And the workaholic undertaker Howard Hodgson, who turned his small Birmingham family firm of undertakers into a public company worth millions, decided it was time to change direction when he hit forty. Hodgson, a proponent of the early morning – the *really* early morning – meeting and the sort of man who held conferences from his hospital room when he was laid up with a bad back, used to share a train with me occasionally from the Midlands, so I was shocked when I heard that he was going to sell his substantial stake in the business to spend more time with his family, which included a new baby daughter. 'I get awfully enthusiastic,' he explained. 'I can't trust myself to keep within sensible bounds. It's all or nothing.'

Although Hodgson had many enthusiasms, from Beatles music to football, I understood that undertaking was in his blood, since he had been a coffin-follower since childhood and pioneered many American-style 'buy now, die later' policies in Britain. But for Hodgson, as for many New Age 'change-of-lifers', 'retirement' is not the be-all and the end-all but the doorway to an even more eventful afterlife. He had no desire to sit twiddling his thumbs. Like Norman Fowler he had several books on the boil, and was on the lookout for non-executive directorships to provide his workaholic nature with new stimuli. Hodgson has already formed his own management consultancy and was, at the time of writing, planning 'a financial services company, setting myself a target to float it in ten years' time. I didn't want to be just remembered as "the enfant terrible who changed funeral directing",' he told me. 'As the chief executive of a public company the company runs you, whereas this way I'll be running things.' Rumours of his retirement, therefore, have been greatly exaggerated – although he does intend to devote a considerable amount of time to charity work, and was preparing to dine with the Prince of Wales about the Prince's Trust as we spoke. 'I'm a very competitive person,' he confided, 'and there is a certain arrogance that you want to be the *best*. Forty just seemed a logical time to change direction.'

Some might return to study – like the top Scotland Yard official I interviewed for an article on mature students at an Oxford college for *The Times* in 1989; at the age of fifty-two he had decided to read philosophy, swapping his official car and senior salary for a bicycle and student grant.

Others might trade in their high-paying, high-prestige job for a home consultancy, like the sixty-hour-a-week manager with a major multinational company who quit to combine the role of family man with a successful career as a home-based management consultant and announced, 'I've proved that you can be successful without sacrificing your family and I feel so much better.' He was able to take his children to school, work flat out for five hours, enjoy afternoons and early evenings with his family and resume work when the children were in bed.

Others might fulfil a lifelong ambition, like the thirty-five-year-old former dealer with a London merchant bank who told one newspaper how much happier he was since quitting his high paying job to become a railwayman, cutting his working week from seventy-eight hours to thirty-nine and his salary by thousands of pounds.

One senior British executive took a 50 per cent salary cut and asked his company for a less demanding job in the provinces, and is currently combining work with research for a PhD in comparative linguistics. As McNulty observed, 'To outer-directed people education is achievement-oriented, but to the inner-directeds, at the leading edge, it is a lifelong process.'

'I was fed up with twelve- and fourteen-hour days,' said Paula Shea, former leisure analyst with a major stockbroking firm who wanted to 'get out', as she puts it, before she was made redundant at the end of the 1980s. At the time of writing she is running her own consultancy and has time 'to see my friends, entertain, and do a course in advanced French, which I would never have had time for before'.

Amanda Walker, thirty-three, is grateful for cutting her professional teeth in Margaret Thatcher's work-aholic Britain. 'The Thatcher years were good to me,' believes the former chartered accountant who 'fast-tracked' her way into a senior post with a major insurance company, which made it clear, she feels, that it didn't think she would be able to stand the pace when she became pregnant.

'Maybe the decision to have a baby in the first place reflected my changing perspective,' Mrs Walker, at the time of writing financial development manager for a county council, reflected to me for an article I was researching on the subject for *The Times*. 'It's not that I've become less ambitious – I'm still very anxious to achieve promotion – but I'm delighted to say that my employer is very forward-looking and the attitude is that if you're committed and conscientious, there's no need to work the sort of ridiculously long hours I used to. They want people to be *fresh*. I used to be in at 8 am and seldom away before 7.30. Now I'm always home at 6 pm and am able to switch off completely to play with my four-year-old son. I have also found time to go to a gym twice a week – which I never had time for before – and take much better care of myself generally.'

Such people as these remain 'work enthusiasts' by finding work to become enthusiastic about when they begin to feel jaded – or new working methods, which allow their enthusiasm to bubble to the surface again. They are as self-motivated about their personal balancing acts as they are in their work. They are not the sort of people who need to wait until divorce or a heart attack forces them to take a closer look at their lives. But a more user-friendly corporate culture is emerging which should make it easier for everyone, even work-ambivalents, to become work enthusiasts.

In the 1980s people were paid high salaries but treated as if they were expendable. Young men and women in their twenties were earning six-figure salaries plus commission in intensely pressured

financial arenas, where the risks were as great as the rewards and they were burnt out before they were thirty.

'Motivational' courses were run like military manoeuvres in which managing directors (yes, honestly!) flew over their sweating staff in helicopters to spot the 'wimps' who weren't up to scratch, and participants ran like hell, knowing there was somebody close behind just panting to fill their shoes. (Motivational marketing establishments were another great growth industry of the 1980s.)

In the 1990s both individuals and organizations – even if only because of demographics – are learning to take a longer-term view. Paula Grayson suggests that this is 'because companies have learned that 70 per cent of their costs are people, and they'd better make the most of them, even if only for purely economic reasons!' Motivation must be of the carrot, not the stick, variety and if square pegs don't fit into round holes a new niche must be carved for them instead of allowing them simply to peg out. John Nicholson is delighted to report that, 'We've had a new assignment this year with a large and totally British corporation which has set us to work trying to find means of spotting now and treating in such a way as they're still with the company in fifteen years people of twenty-four with directorial potential. That's a real shift in thinking.'

It must never be forgotten that necessity is the mother of invention. When women were needed to 'man' the munitions factories during the Second World War, the country was fed a quick and comprehensive dose of propaganda about how easily women could do men's jobs – and how healthy it was for children to be put into crèches. Then when jobs were needed for returning men, the working woman was made to feel guilty and the crèches which had made possible her wartime effort were disbanded and condemned. When it was first mooted, a few years ago, that by the year 2000 nearly 16 per cent of the population would be over sixty-five, there would be 1 million Britons over eighty-five and a diminishing younger population to support them, companies began to work on ways of finding useful employment for the elderly.

According to one American survey, people don't retire to stop working but to gain more control over how they spend their time. Give them this and most people would enjoy working part-time, it concluded. A few companies, such as the DIY chain B&Q, began staffing certain stores entirely with over-fifties and discovered that older people not only had a better knowledge of what they were selling but a more winning way with customers.

Only this year a major battle has been won against ageism through upper age limits in job advertisements, although a Gallup poll discovered that nearly nine out of ten British employers discriminated against the over-thirty-fives and only one in six was prepared to consider anyone over fifty.

At the same time early-retirement programmes, once only a euphemism for redundancy or a perk of a few high-achievers, are becoming more widely available to make sure that no one is forced to stay on at work reluctantly and resentfully. Many big companies now have a retirement age of fifty-five for their senior executives, which leaves them with plenty of life to take on new directorships and explore new avenues of endeavour (or enjoy the young, second families they have so often acquired, like Sir Norman Fowler, along the way).

Work enthusiasts would argue that those who want to stay on at work until they are sixty-five or older should be allowed to, health and faculties permitting, at least part-time – and Age Concern England, in its publication *Age: Unrecognized Discrimination* (1991), suggests that older employees can make valuable mentors to young bosses.

Would anyone have stopped Leonard Bernstein from conducting at sixty-five, Picasso from painting, the septuagenarian Lord Weidenfeld from pursuing his jet-setting life as a transatlantic publisher and partygoer, the veteran photographer Eve Arnold from travelling the world with her camera or the venerable Alan Whicker from broadcasting? And look at Barbara Cartland, at nearly ninety still able to produce a novel every couple of weeks and answer 40,000 letters a year while campaigning for 'wages for wives' and other pet projects in the process.

My own father, a manager of concert and opera artists' careers, who worked – like most workaholic New Yorkers – until he died, in harness, in his mid-seventies, would have withered away in an enforced retirement. My mother, at the time of writing, still runs her own highly creative business at an age she would not thank me for revealing.

From the regretful way one recently retired local government officer spoke of the sudden jolt of leaving a highly pressured, high-power job for the dubious delights of pottering around the house doing the decorating, it is clear that new ways of weaving together different working patterns, skills and desires must be a future priority, so that everyone can work according to his or her ambitions and abilities. Phased-out retirement, like phased-in return to work for women coming back after a baby, is obviously desirable.

Somewhere around the turn of the decade it was discovered that people were a precious and, it was predicted, an increasingly rare commodity, and that – in the words of one ex-workaholic who got off the treadmill without falling off the fast track – 'You really only get to pass through this life once. This is not a practice run.' A new generation of 'caring' companies began to evolve – some truly inner-directed, others reaching similar conclusions and practices with less altruistic motives.

Changes have already been dramatic among

companies with reputations as high-stress employers creating corporate clones and drones. Some may have been implemented out of fear. 'Employers are running scared,' John Nicholson suggests. 'They look at demographic trends and the increasingly sophisticated expectations of their customers and realize they had better start getting their employees interested in what they're doing before it's too late.' But they are still on the right track.

IBM, for example, is living down its fast-track treadmill reputation and the joke that IBM stood for 'I've Been Moved', because it demanded so much stressful mobility from its executives. It offers creative brain training, flexible working hours – so that employees must be at their desks only at a 'core' time of between 9.45 am and 4.20 pm and can log on any time after 7 pm – and a relocation package which now includes preliminary visits and sophisticated support services. And it is a rare major multinational today that doesn't make use of some aspect of 'corporate counselling', a lucrative industry (with specialists getting thousands of pounds a day) which can provide group seminars and private counselling on anything from assertiveness and colour coordination, to time management and how to cope with the trauma of frequent relocations.

A doctor wrote a letter to *The Times* in 1988, complaining of the divorce and delinquency, psychological and psychosomatic problems which he believed marked the downward spiral of upward mobility. One man I talked to in order to follow this up had moved three times in six years as a television company executive; another had been moved nine times in twenty years before deciding to start up his own relocation counselling service to help minimize the strain for others.

According to a survey of 500 workplaces published by the Labour Research Department at the end of 1989, one in five employers provided stress counselling and 56 per cent of staff questioned would have liked such a service to be available. Already, I am confident, both figures have substantially risen. As one counsellor told the *Sunday Times* at the time, 'British managers used to suffer the John Wayne syndrome – it was a sign of weakness to acknowledge stress. Now the medical profession has shown that stress is one of the factors in many illnesses and people are realizing that if it affects your life, surely it also affects your work.'

Employees whose firms offer counselling services are encouraged to use them independently and in complete privacy – but many, understandably, mistrust promises of confidentiality and are unlikely to tell someone they regard as a mouthpiece (and possible earpiece) of their boss that they don't feel they're up to the job – or that they're having, say, sexual problems at home.

Dr David Lewis – frequently called in to counsel companies or to give workshops on channelling stress creatively – warns against those which are cynically making use of experts like himself as a sop to their guilty consciences.

'I am not happy,' he says, 'to perform a mopping-up operation in companies which put too many stresses on their employees and think, because they call me in, that makes it all right. They also have to be prepared to change.'

Anne Wilson Schaef is scornful of making a great play of minor changes when really a complete and radical overhaul is required. 'Most organizations say they want to be innovative and change,' she writes in *The Addictive Organization*. 'We find that they mean "making changes" rather than change. The controlled element of "making changes" can often result in a "fix" for the organization. It gives the illusion that something is happening when, in reality, the change is avoiding any significant activity.'

Admittedly we are in a transitional stage, but most people favour evolution rather than revolution, and since many British companies have not yet quite reached the addictive stage of some of the American ones she describes, a gentler process may be appropriate.

Lord Sieff, chairman of that caring company Marks & Spencer – which provides its employees with subsidized food, hairdressing and shares in the company, as well as making an effort to care about the environment – wrote in *Marcus Sieff on Management* (Weidenfeld & Nicholson, 1990), 'It is a combination of the guidance of the businessman and the energy of the cooperative worker, and not the state, which should create the national wealth necessary to provide real social progress, proper social security and true social care.'

The old values of 'paternalistic' management propounded by Lord Sieff are being dusted off and updated and almost every day British newspapers publish encouraging stories about innovative working practices, such as plans for crèches and paternity leave and flexible hours and office facilities on trains. Yet – sometimes on the same page – these same newspapers carry conflicting reports which demonstrate the extent of confusion which exists over working attitudes, practices and prognoses for the 1990s. It seems to be both the best of times and the worst of times.

One day in January 1991 the same page of the same newspaper – *Today* – carried an article reporting that working mothers were to be given a £30 a week cash bonus by one of the water authorities as a ploy to get them to stay at work, while another reported that, 'The number of people out of work rose by more than 80,000 in December [1990] . . . secretaries, computer operators and senior managers have all seen "safe" jobs go to the wall as the recession bites.'

Despite jobs disappearing, workers are becoming more discriminating – and not just white-collar workers. On the last day of 1990 the *Financial Times* announced that, 'Unions are now attaching shorter-hours claims to almost every pay submission', and that 'the first sign that the thirty-seven-hour working week is spreading from the engineering and water sectors across British industry has emerged in an offer to unions from Rowntree Mackintosh', which had agreed in principle to a thirty-seven-hour week for certain workers. And there have been increasingly insistent 'noises off' about lowering the hours worked by junior hospital doctors too drugged by lack of sleep to administer the right doses – and turning Parliament into a 9 to 5-ish job, abandoning the late-night sittings to allow MPs a greater opportunity for home life, even if the new hours make it more difficult to deal with the lucrative outside interests on which many have come to depend.

Encouraging moves have been made – spearheaded by the Health Minister Virginia Bottomley (with her husband, Peter, another inspirationally workaholic husband and wife political team) – to introduce part-time training posts to help women doctors on the way up combine a career with a family. 'Women training in surgical specialities will be identified and receive the support and encouragement they need to enable them to become consultants,' she said – a move the Government was supporting to the tune of £1.5 million.

Yet women venturing forth to find the 'brave new world' of opportunities they have been promised now awaits them after a 'career break' to raise children find only doors slamming rudely in their faces, shattering their fragile confidence. Many women wrote to *The Times* about their disappointing experiences in the job market after having been psyched up by all the propaganda about the new importance of women in the workplace, and encouraged by the profusion of courses for potential 'women returners' on everything from management style to personal style.

'One man said he wouldn't interview any woman with two children because she wouldn't be able to work late – even though my two are teenagers and away at boarding school,' one recalled. 'I was in one young company where I was very much older than everyone I was working for and I got the distinct feeling it made them uncomfortable,' said another.

Paula Grayson explained, 'People are thinking in macro-terms and then they encounter micro-problems.' (Small comfort to those who have been told they'll be needed in a few years' time but are rejected now!) But that was before the recession which began to bite at the beginning of 1991. As this book goes to press every day's papers announce new company closures and massive staff cuts. I fear we're about to hear the propaganda machine grind noisily into

reverse, persuading women that they'd be better off
with Barbara Cartland's 'Wages for Wives' than tax
relief on childcare to enable them to go out to work.

And where will those wages – or that tax relief –
come from with Government spending so tight?

On the plus side, however, job-sharing, flexitime
and tele-working facilities should continue to make it
easier to incorporate women returners, pensioners
and all sorts of part-timers into the working network,
and will no doubt account for some of the additional
ten hours a week leisure time the Henley Centre
predicted, in 1990, we would all be enjoying by the end
of the decade.

As *Fortune* magazine advised its readers, 'Don't
demand that all work be done at the office: reward
good workers with computers and telecommunications
devices so they can work at home'. Bosses will find
that this investment repays itself many times over,
since – as with job-sharing or any new working
scheme which gives more freedom and flexibility to
participants – enthusiastic workers will double their
efforts to prove its efficacy. The danger is that
workaholic home-workers may find it difficult to
switch off.

Fortune sums up the clashing work ethics of this
tempestuously transitional period when it notes that
'Apple Computer [*sic*] is more sensitive than most
companies to the stress that comes with overwork – it
offers massage on the premises, sponsors an equestrian
club, and gives aikido lessons to help workers blow off
steam. But the manager at Apple who came to work a
couple of days after she gave birth last year was not
sent home.' It concludes that, 'The hard job of not
working so hard is up to you', and proceeds to offer

suggestions to would-be skivers on how to 'join philanthropic or professional organizations that have been blessed by the company', since 'getting a seat on the National Footwear Council won't be seen by your superiors as running away from work', or how to 'take up exercise in your lunch hour', because 'unless your boss is prepared to confess that he doesn't care if you drop dead at your desk, he can hardly argue . . .'

For workaholics, however, the 'boss' is an inner drive to work that won't be fobbed off by feeble excuses. But we must learn to shed some of the deadwood from our working lives so that we can turn to the tasks we really need – and want – to do with renewed enthusiasm and creative energy. For some that may simply mean cutting down on commuting time – an enticing concept cunningly capitalized upon by at least one firm of property developers, who recently placed an advertisement in newspapers with the word WORKAHOLICS in huge letters, promising, 'We've got just the thing for you! Why rent expensive premises when you can work *and* expand from home?'

The idea was that you would move to Melville Homes' Family Enterprise Homes at Coggeshall, Essex ('starting from only £89,950') – 'a combination of a new three- or four-bedroom home with fully equipped business premises – either detached or part of the home'. You even got a 'free business starter pack' of 'fax, ansaphone and photocopier already installed and waiting to start work'. At a time when properties were hardly moving, business rents (and rail fares) were soaring and thousands of redundant employees were on the brink of enforced entrepreneurship, it made a tempting package – particularly with '100 per cent market value on part exchange'.

But targeting workaholics was a curious marketing ploy in the changing climate. The workaholic drone of the 1980s is already an endangered species. The work-ambivalent will continue to compose the vast majority of the workforce. But the work enthusiast must be in the vanguard of change, providing the inspiration and leadership needed, Christine McNulty is convinced, in the new millennium – occasionally forgoing balance in the quest for excellence.

Less inspired workaholics will need to spot the changes and change their spots – a process which will not happen overnight. Shock tactics may be necessary in some cases, but people *can* change.

When I interviewed a number of former hostages and their families for an article in *Good Housekeeping* in 1990, I was surprised by the way so many of them insisted that having been held hostage was one of the best things that could have happened to them because it irrevocably altered their priorities.

Georges Hanson, a once-workaholic French television cameraman seized by Iranian Shi'ite extremists in Beirut in 1986, summed up the general feeling when he told me, 'When I was a prisoner I had regrets that I had not profited as much as I could have from the time spent with my family, and I determined to do things differently when I returned. Now I take much more pleasure in being in the country, in spending time with friends – and I no longer *aspire* the way I used to, professionally or materially.'

He still loved his work, he still travelled, but whereas once he wouldn't think to phone his family and would 'cut himself off from family concerns', his wife recalled, 'now he calls frequently'. They agree that he's 'a much happier person now' than in his earlier, workaholic incarnation.

When a workaholic senior executive officer at the Office of Population Censuses and Surveys was found dead in his fume-filled car in 1990, having worked seven days a week, sometimes until two o'clock in the morning, his widow told the inquest how 'his career was his life. I got sick of hearing about the 1991 census!' The coroner, recording an open verdict, cautioned the court in words which I feel make a fitting ending to this book and epitaph to an era.

'We live in times when working hard is very fashionable,' the coroner, Tim Milligan, said. 'We are constantly urged that it is necessary in the nation's interests. I am sure it is. But there is also a significant danger that we will get this out of context. We have, after all, only one life. The world is a wonderfully rich place to live, with much to offer outside work. We should have energy and attention not only for work and career, but also for our families.'

We must not prostrate ourselves at the altar of work, nor sacrifice our humanity upon it – although it can offer many blessings. If we can love our work without forgetting that we have to work on our love too, we should be better able to work everything out.

A Personal Postscript

'Work and thou wilt bless the day,
Ere the toil be done;
They that work not cannot pray
Cannot feel the sun.
God is living, working still,
All things work and move;
Work or lose the power to will,
Lose the power to love.'
John Sullivan Dwight

My six-year-old daughter told a friend that she wanted to be a journalist just like me. 'What's a journalist?' the friend asked. 'It's a thing that types all the time,' said my daughter. Then she went off to play at having 'important work' to do and I heard her telling her dollies to 'Shhh . . .' as she was very busy.

This was sufficient to make me pause long enough to pay attention to the piece of paper my nine-year-old son came into my office waving. He was proudly showing me the computer graphic he had designed of a person at a desk overflowing with papers, entitled 'workaholic'. It was for me.

These two incidents, both of which occurred while I was writing this book, together with what I was learning while writing the book, made me wonder whether it was time for *me* to slow down a bit, take stock and reassess my own priorities.

I have never had the slightest guilt about being a working mother – or contemplated any other choice. I feel women have as much right to work for self-fulfilment as men do and was raised in a family – dysfunctional or not – in which such a truth was held to be self-evident. For me that fulfilment has always come largely from work, and I cannot imagine it any other way.

Business trips or lengthy working days away from home have never bothered me if I know my children are in good hands – nor, I'm happy to say, do they ever seem to have bothered *them*, accustomed, as they were, to my absences so early. I could never understand those clingy children who cried when they were prised off their parents' knees to go into nursery school.

But I was beginning to feel guilty about not being 100 per cent with my children when I was *with* them. I found myself always saying, 'in a minute', and that minute would never quite come, or 'not now', until I began asking myself, 'If not now, then *when*?'

I began to consider, like Norman Fowler, that you couldn't take children down from a shelf after ten years like an unfinished book. On the other hand, of course, the book might still be there in ten years, a source of pride and possible support to me in my old age, while my children could, like those of a friend of mine who gave up her career to devote herself to them, have washed their hands of me by then.

And one of my non-working friends told me she felt

similarly guilty about 'switching-off' to her children because she always seemed to have something around the house to do, so this is not a phenomenon unique to workaholics.

That said, my personal recipe for a more balanced life – which I *mean* to try to keep to as soon as I've finished this book – is to try to be wholeheartedly and 100 per cent with whatever or whomever I've decided to be with for the moment.

As someone who likes to exercise while reading a newspaper and watching television at the same time (and calls that *'quality time'* with the children!), this could be difficult, but I suspect the results will be worth it.

I think I will also resolve never to write another book – at least not until I'm old and famous enough to write my memoirs or daring enough to embark on a sexy novel. Because as a workaholic *journalist*, writing this book was sheer torture, since I found that to switch off from the day-to-day cut and thrust of newspaper writing and immerse myself in a single subject for so long was alien to my nature. Each day I'd read the newspapers and be bubbling over with ideas for stories I wanted to write – and it was very frustrating not to be able to suggest them and to keep my involvement at a minimum. (So a workaholic is not workaholic about *all* kinds of work, but is, in fact, very selective about choosing something suitable to his or her abilities and enthusiasms.)

Fortunately, as a fairly prolific and productive workaholic, that period didn't last too long!

While admittedly seeking a better balance in my own life, I harbour a secret and probably unworthy suspicion that juggling is more exciting. I wonder whether the pursuit of perfect balance will become a new obsession, even more all-consuming than work-aholism. And whether in the process we may lose the jagged irregularity of genius and erratic spurts of creativity.

In our eagerness to create a balanced working environment, with balanced employees leading balanced lives, divided equally between work and family commitments, each taking their (strictly enforced) holiday, isn't there a danger that some of the enthusiasm and drive that characterizes an unbalanced, workaholic commitment may be lost along the way?

Of course, I'm playing the Devil's advocate. But I'd rather see my children knowing what they want to do in life and busying themselves, as they have done since they were very young, with 'important' projects than whining, 'I'm bored!' and, later, in life, bumbling around with a vague urge to 'find' themselves.

'Press cuttings won't keep you warm when you're old,' a woman who, it was generally acknowledged, was a very great opera singer once gave as her reason for letting her career take second place to her family and consequently become second-rate. But there's no guarantee that children will either. They've got their own lives to lead, and if you've given up what you consider to be a vital part of yours for them, don't expect them to thank you for the sacrifice.

As for other people, well, as Shakespeare advised, 'to thine own self be true, / And it must follow, as the night the day, / 'Thou canst not then be false to any man.'

For true work enthusiasts, being true to yourself means continuing to work with enjoyment and absorption well into old age. Only if the enjoyment disappears and the absorption becomes an obsession do we need to worry. And who's got time to worry?